financial literacy
doodle
notebook

doodle notes®

learning benefits of visual note-taking

stronger
focus

retention
through
dual coding

mental
connections

memory
boost

communication
between
brain
hemispheres

building
long-term
memories

activated
neural
pathways

increased
creativity
& alertness

associative
recognition

picture
superiority
effect

relaxation
benefits

problem
solving
skills boost

Thanks so much for purchasing this book!

Thanks and credit to the following artists:

To learn more about the doodle note® method and download your free Doodle Note Handbook, visit

doodlenotes.org

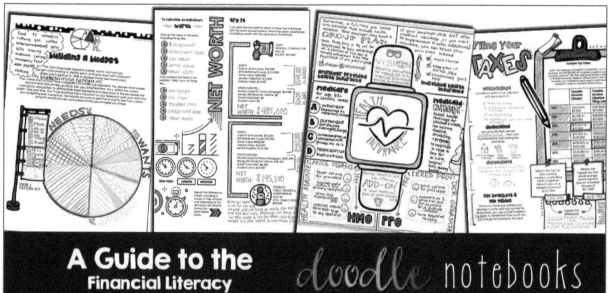

A Guide to the
Financial Literacy
doodle notebooks

doodle notes®

learning benefits of visual note-taking

The brain processes linguistic input (teacher voice, written text, words) in a completely different area from all graphic input. But when visual or graphic input is BLENDED with the words, the two regions of the brain connect.

The referential connections between the two zones allow the information to actually be stored and become long-term memory!

This is called Dual Coding Theory.

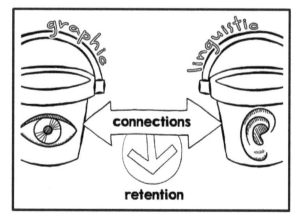

doodling **takes just enough**

attention to keep the brain from daydreaming without allowing it to become distracted.

doodlenotes.org

It has been proven that students can retain more information when they connect the linguistic and visual centers of the brain.

Doodling while listening has also been proven to improve focus! Visual note methods have numerous benefits for student learning.

doodle notebook

What's Included?

Introductory Pages:
to model the method while showing students WHY visual note-taking engages the brain

Chapter Cover Pages
Just for fun & organization!
(Students can color if they want to)

doodle notebook

What's Included?

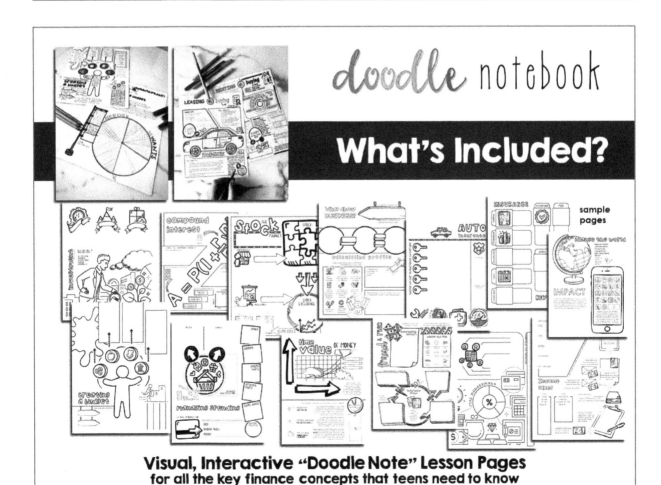

Visual, Interactive "Doodle Note" Lesson Pages
for all the key finance concepts that teens need to know

doodle notebook

What's Included?

10 Blank Templates
for adding any extra lesson topics you'd like students to have included

This way everything will be in one place instead of additional notes being on loose paper (and still with the brain-based benefits of the visual note format!)

Answer Keys & Photo Samples
for guided note-taking

---

doodle notebook

What makes the "doodle note" method effective?

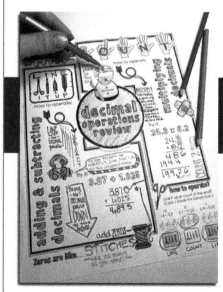

A unique blend of...

✓ visual memory triggers / graphic analogies

✓ interactive tasks

✓ student input

visual memory trigger

a blend of teacher input and plenty of space for student input

graphic analogy

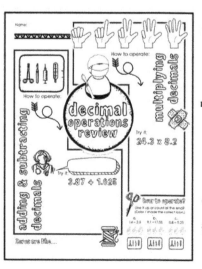

visual memory trigger

interactive task

opportunities to color, doodle, embellish, and do hand-lettering

contents

contents

GUIDED AUDIO LECTURE & FULL SIZE COLORED SAMPLES FOR EACH PAGE ARE AVAILABLE AT MATHGIRAFFE.COM/SUPPLEMENT

ENGAGE your brain!
- doodle, sketch, color -

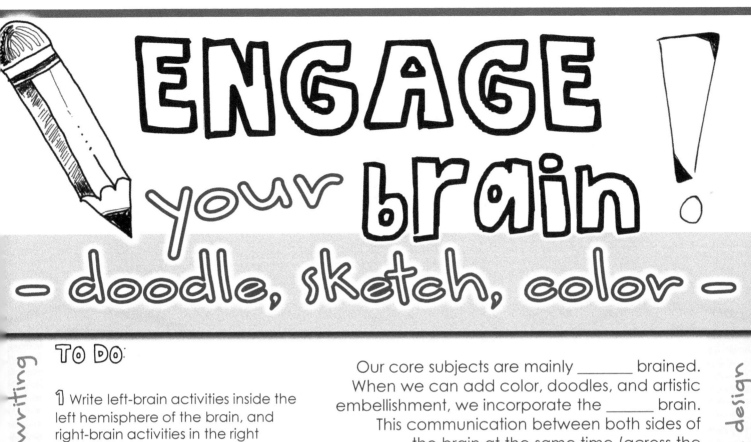

TO DO:

1 Write left-brain activities inside the left hemisphere of the brain, and right-brain activities in the right hemisphere.

2 Choose 9 of the brain benefits to write on the lines.

3 Label the corpus callosum.

Our core subjects are mainly _____ brained. When we can add color, doodles, and artistic embellishment, we incorporate the _____ brain. This communication between both sides of the brain at the same time (across the _____ _____) activates our brains more fully to help us to maximize:

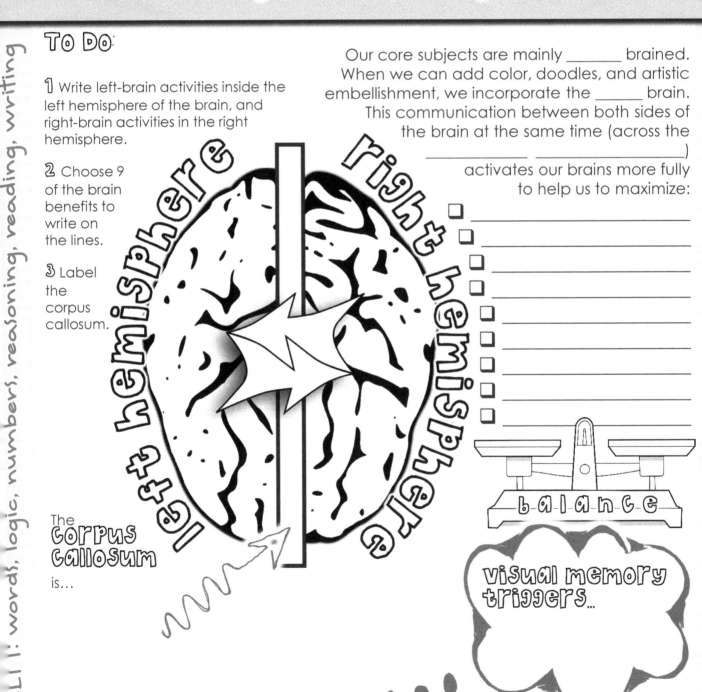

- _____
- _____
- _____
- _____
- _____
- _____
- _____
- _____
- _____

balance

left hemisphere

right hemisphere

The corpus callosum is...

visual memory triggers...

LEFT: words, logic, numbers, reasoning, reading, writing

RIGHT: color, music, art, visual, spatial, creative, design

brain processing

The brain processes new learned material in two completely separate areas! Label the types of input that enter each center of the brain.

Name:

graphic

linguistic

But, to convert the information to long-term memory (actually LEARN it), we need to _____ the two!

retention

Taking visual notes helps us to

blend

& _____

learning benefits of visual note-taking

stronger **focus**

retention through dual coding

mental connections

communication between **brain** hemispheres

building long-term memories

activated **neural** pathways

memory **boost**

associative recognition

relaxation **benefits**

increased **creativity** & alertness

picture superiority **effect**

problem solving skills boost

Banking & Budgeting Basics

A savings account...

Inside the piggy bank, doodle some examples of purchases that you'd have to pull from your savings account for as an adult.

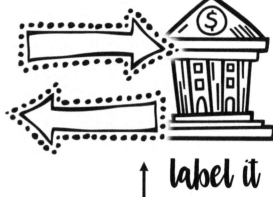

label it

What do you call a transaction that puts money into your account? What about taking money out?

How does putting your money in a bank benefit you?

1

2

How does the bank benefit?

What fees might a bank charge?

fees

banking accounts

•BA

compare it

savings

checking

investment

What is a CD?

Your checking account works more like a _____ that you can access daily for:

Inside the coin purse above, doodle or write some examples of day-to-day purchases that you'd use your checking account for, rather than pulling from your savings account each day as an adult.

doodle it

What are some challenges / barriers that could keep you from saving enough money?

BANK

strategize

How can you improve saving habits?

Started with $512

Wrote $350 check

Deposited $425

Spent $18 (Debit)

Paid $45 bill

Withdrew $80

Find the balance of a bank account with the transactions listed in the coin stack →

Balance:

color code

Mark additions (positive) in blue and deductions (negative) in red.

DEFINE EACH:

principal

interest rate

interest

Simple interest

EXPLAIN IT:

MAP OUT HOW IT WORKS:

FILL IT IN:

$$I = prt$$

simple interest
USING THE FORMULA

I = prt

17

label it

Use hand lettering to place each of these terms somewhere in the correct area of the flowchart and explain.

- ☐ Withholdings
- ☐ Tips
- ☐ Extra / Entertainment
- ☐ Paycheck
- ☐ Work
- ☐ Food, Medical, & Other Needs
- ☐ Savings
- ☐ Gross Pay
- ☐ Home expenses and bills
- ☐ Net Pay
- ☐ Benefits

doodle it

Draw an icon to represent each type of withholding:

taxes

social security

medicare

retirement

medical insurance

earning a paycheck

employer match

When you contribute to your own _____ retirement plan, some employers will _____ up to a certain percentage with their own contribution.

Different education levels can give you access to different careers. However, many students have _____ from college loans. Weigh your options. Trades often pay well too. Jobs at which you earn _____ or _____ may have lower base pay.

education

reading a paycheck

1519

Pay to the order of: _____

Two thousand two hundred fifty-three and 56/100 dollars   **$2,253.56**

Pay Period: Dec. 1 through Dec. 14, 2015	**Total Earnings**	**Withholdings**	
		Federal Tax:	$513.25
pretend paycheck: math purposes only	**$3121.14**	Social Security:	$256.19
		Medicare:	$98.14

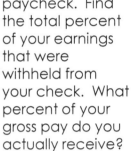

try it

Compare the gross pay and net pay on this simplified sample paycheck. Find the total percent of your earnings that were withheld from your check. What percent of your gross pay do you actually receive?

Assume that the paycheck shown here is the first one you receive for a new career with consistent income. To kick off a good savings habit with your new income, you plan to deposit one paycheck (half of your first month's income, since each month you earn two paychecks) into an account with simple interest. The interest rate is 2.25%. Calculate the total amount that you would have in the account after 10 years.

In the box, write or draw cases that may require you to access your emergency fund.

doodle it

Creating an Emergency Fund

Experts recommend keeping three months worth of expenses in an account as an emergency savings that you never touch unless you have to. Assuming that you earn the paycheck shown above every two weeks, calculate approximately how much you should save in your emergency fund.

compound interest

Interest rate goes into the formula in _____ format.

$$A = P\left(1 + \frac{r}{n}\right)^{nt}$$

SIMPLE VS. COMPOUND INTEREST

What's the difference?

What's included in the balance?

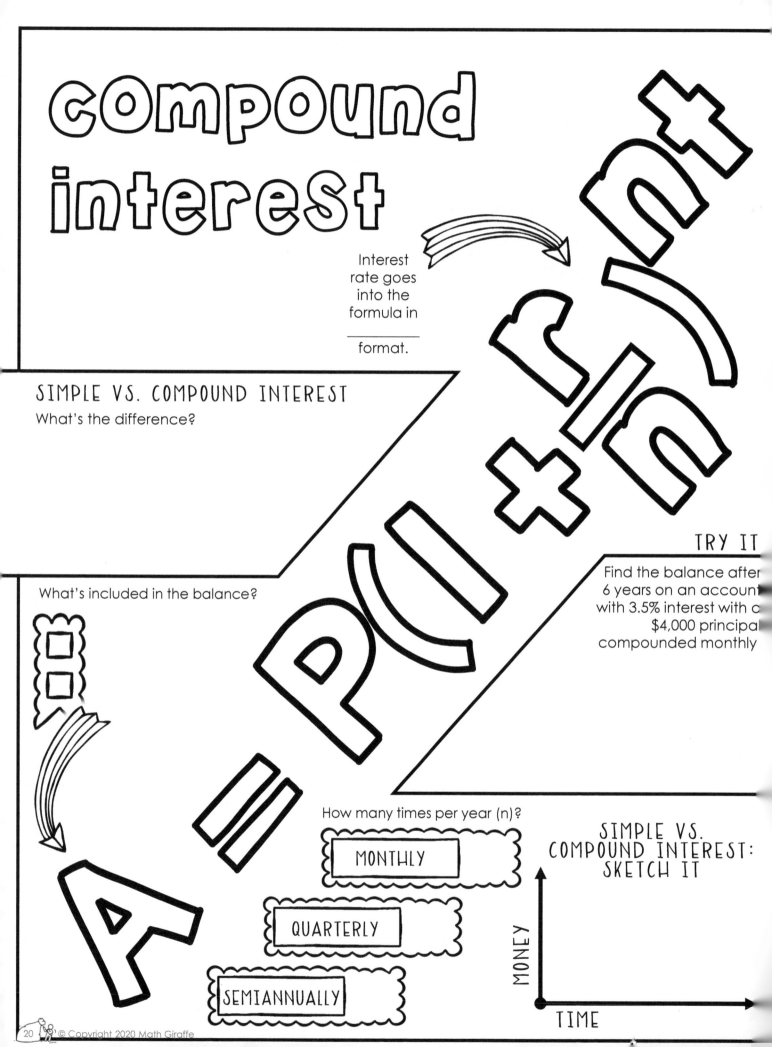

TRY IT

Find the balance after 6 years on an account with 3.5% interest with a $4,000 principal compounded monthly

How many times per year (n)?

- MONTHLY
- QUARTERLY
- SEMIANNUALLY

SIMPLE VS. COMPOUND INTEREST: SKETCH IT

MONEY

TIME

NEEDS | WANTS

DELAYED GRATIFICATION

managing spending

debt

asset

debit card

credit card

cash back

EXAMPLE TIPS/FEES

EXTRAS TO BUDGET FOR:

These expenses may be added on top of the cost of goods / services.

tip

sales tax

fees

21

Simple Interest:

$$I = p \cdot r \cdot t$$

where I is the interest accumulated, p is the principal (starting) amount, r is the interest rate in decimal form, and t is time in years. The interest you have earned is then added to the principal at the end of the year.

Compound Interest:

$$A = P(1 + \frac{r}{n})^{nt}$$

where A is the final value, P is the principal (initial value), r is the interest rate in decimal form, n is the number of times per year that the interest is compounded, and t is the number of years invested.

Calculating interest

Interest can work ...

Kye sets up a small investment at age 22 to send just $3,000 of his income into a fund that earns an average of 10% interest (compounded monthly). How much money will be in this account when he wants to use the money when he turns 70?

Reno wants to furnish his new apartment, but only has gotten one paycheck so far. He purchased furniture with a credit card, spending $2100.00 total. He waited six months to pay this off, and the credit card company charges 18% interest, compounded daily. How much will that furniture cost him? Fill in the speech bubble with his thoughts upon realizing this.

for you

or

against you

Now find the difference in the final value if he had not done this until he was 30. Draw an emotion on the face to represent how you feel about the difference.

Myah went to trade school and earned a small salary as an apprentice during her education. Now, she is starting her career as an electrician without any debt. She will earn $55,000 per year as her starting salary. She assumes that 30% of her income will go toward taxes, retirement, etc. She then will put 10% of her take-home pay into savings. Knowing that she will have other expenses, she plans to spend only 25% of her net pay on housing. How much should she budget for her rent/mortgage?

2 compare it

1 calculate it

Myah

Jen

Jen accumulated $45,000 in college debt. Now, she is starting her career in IT support. She will earn $65,000 per year as her starting salary. She assumes that 30% of her income will go toward taxes, retirement, etc. She then will put 10% of her take-home pay into savings. What percent of her net pay would she have to budget for housing to be Myah's roommate, splitting the rent/mortgage equally?

Food budget is often around 11% of a person's total take-home pay. Find Jen's food budget and Myah's food budget.

balancing income and expenses

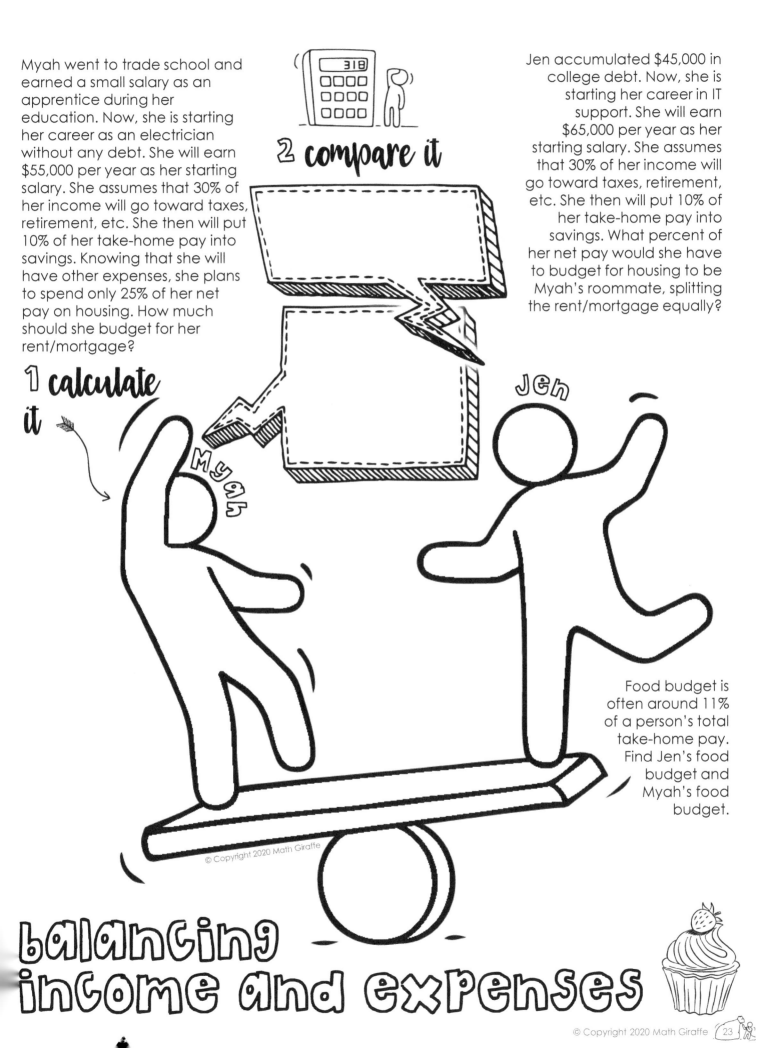

creating a budget

two popular options:

steps to success

3
2
1

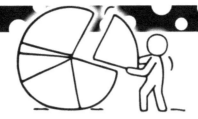

building a budget

First, form three large segments (needs, wants, and savings).
Use light color shading to identify each, and label each with a percent.
(Make sure it adds up to 100% to represent total take-home pay!)

Then, break each of your three categories into smaller sub-segments. You decide what smaller percent each should take up (food, bills, gas, entertainment, etc.). Within the correct color group, add pattern to differentiate these segments and label each in the key beside the graph. Take your time. Don't miss anything that is important to you! Research costs and verify that your budgeting plan is practical. Test real-life amounts of take-home pay to see if your dollar amounts would actually work based on the percentages you chose.

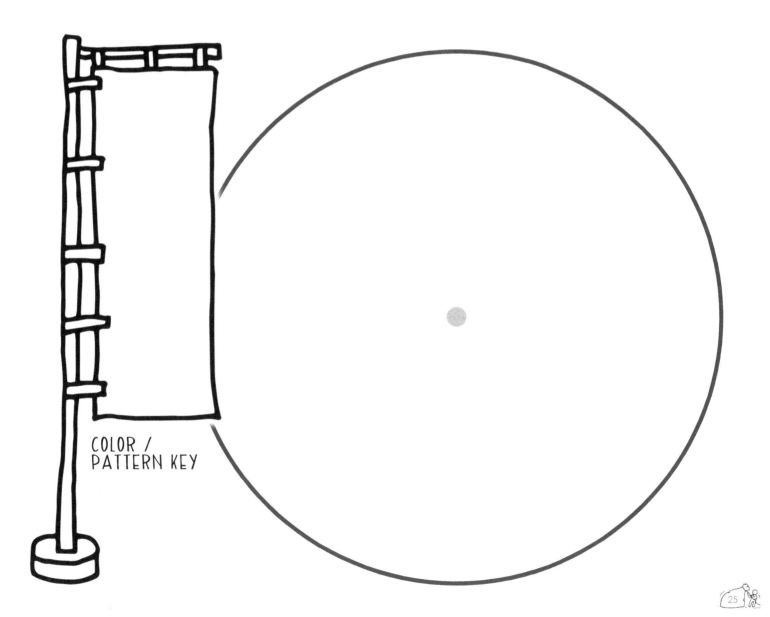

COLOR /
PATTERN KEY

food   TV   cosmetics
clothing   gas   coffee
entertainment(out)   gifts
bills   housing
medicine   savings
emergency fund
debt payoff
clothing   Ooo brainstorming categories

© Copyright 2020 Math Giraffe

building a budget

First, form three large segments (needs, wants, and savings).
Use light color shading to identify each, and label each with a percent.
(Make sure it adds up to 100% to represent total take-home pay!)

Then, break each of your three categories into smaller sub-segments. You decide what smaller percent each should take up (food, bills, gas, entertainment, etc.). Within the correct color group, add pattern to differentiate these segments and label each in the key beside the graph. Take your time. Don't miss anything that is important to you! Research costs and verify that your budgeting plan is practical. Test real-life amounts of take-home pay to see if your dollar amounts would actually work based on the percentages you chose.

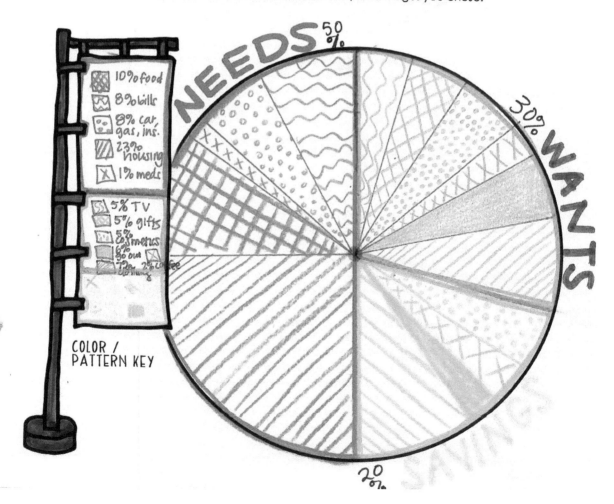

COLOR / PATTERN KEY

2

Investing

investment

Label and explain.

KEY FACTORS TO UNDERSTAND:

- ☐ TIMELINE
- ☐ GOALS
- ☐ % RETURN
- ☐ RISK
- ☐ GROWTH

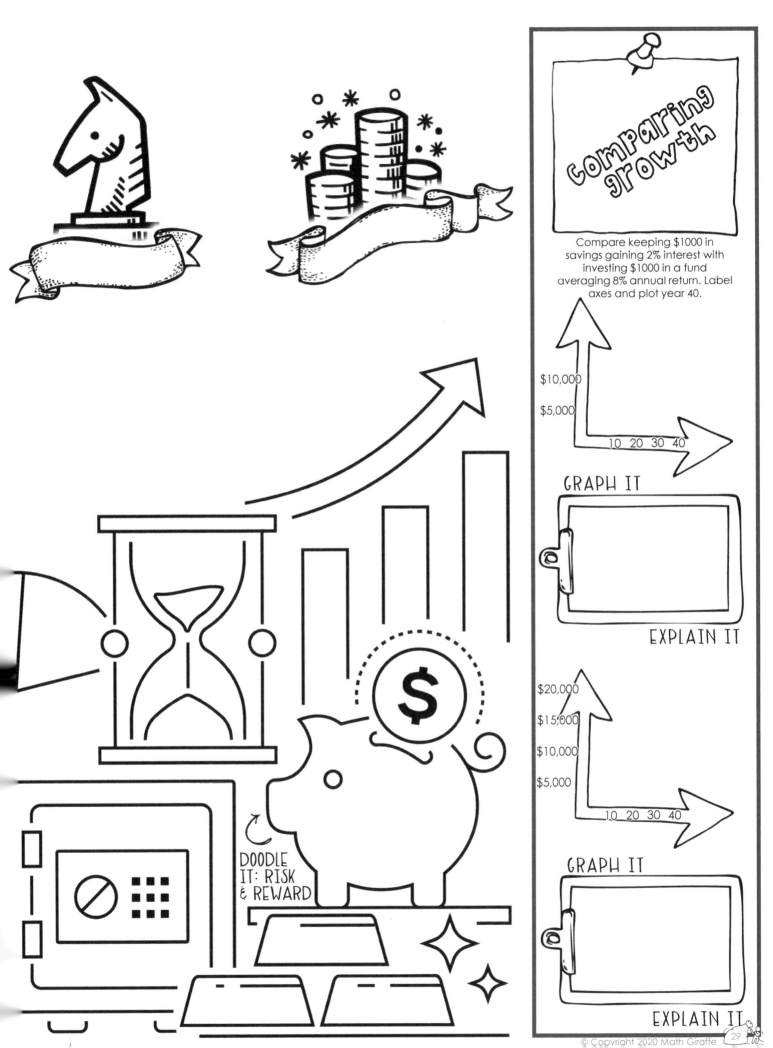

Comparing growth

Compare keeping $1000 in savings gaining 2% interest with investing $1000 in a fund averaging 8% annual return. Label axes and plot year 40.

$10,000
$5,000
10 20 30 40

GRAPH IT

EXPLAIN IT

$20,000
$15,000
$10,000
$5,000
10 20 30 40

GRAPH IT

EXPLAIN IT

DOODLE IT: RISK & REWARD

Color code each segment, draw icons or illustrations to represent each type of investment, and explain.

types of investment

diversification

STOCK

THE STOCK **MARKET**

STOCK:

COMPANIES

INVESTORS

STOCK EXCHANGE

SELLING STOCK

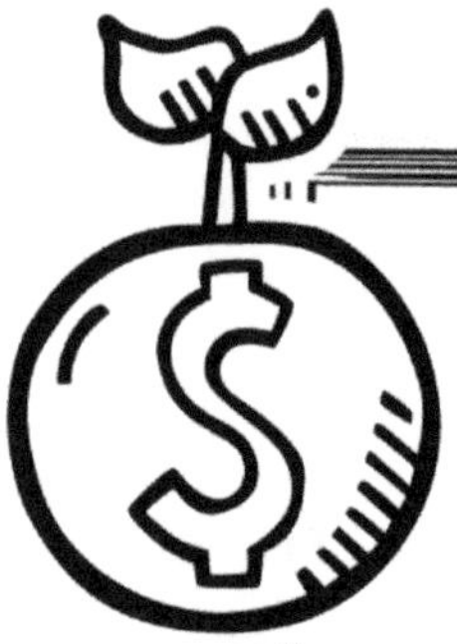

HOW RETIREMENT ACCOUNTS WORK:

401(K)	TRADITIONAL IRA	ROTH IRA

Set up by:

Benefits:

Choice in investing:

VARIATIONS ON 401(K)

BOTH 401(K) AND TRADITIONAL IRA:

Before age 59½ :

After age 70½ :

retirement

When you are saving money for a long period of time (to be used ______________________________), you can often benefit from investing it. There are a lot of options for retirement portfolios. Sometimes your place of employment has a plan set up for you as a _________. Whether or not they do, you can also usually supplement or add your own IRA ____________________________) instead (or in addition).

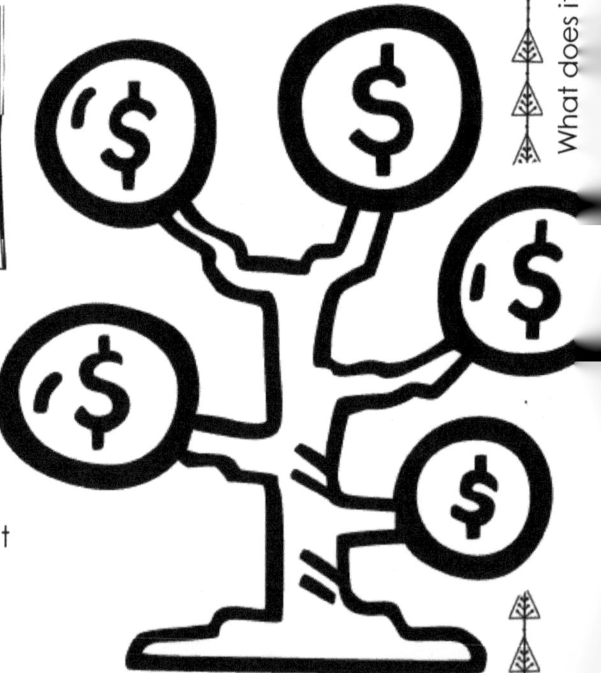

What does it mean for taxes to be **DEFERRED**?

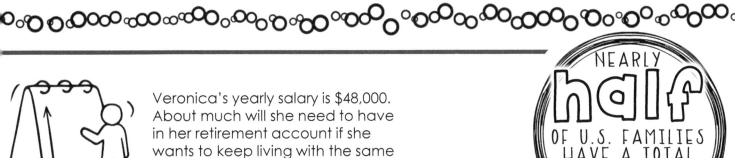

Veronica's yearly salary is $48,000. About much will she need to have in her retirement account if she wants to keep living with the same expenses she has now? (see chart)

NEARLY **half** OF U.S. FAMILIES HAVE A TOTAL RETIREMENT SAVINGS OF **$0**

Planning for retirement

Set a goal for yourself. By age 35, what amount do you think would be a good total retirement savings to have already accumulated?

$480 WAS THE MEDIAN TOTAL RETIREMENT SAVINGS IN 2013 (AGES 32-37)

	Total Saved in Retirement Account	Yearly Income During Retirement
Estimated $ needed	$750,000	$30,000
	$1,000,000	$40,000
	$1,250,000	
	$1,500,000	$60,000
	$1,750,000	$70,000
		$80,000
	$2,250,000	$90,000

These numbers will vary and are not exact. The estimates are just a sample.

Estimate how much retirement savings you'd need to retire and keep your lifestyle if you earn $85,000 as a salary by the end of your working years.

Which of the facts in circles scared you the most? Color from darkest to lightest.

EVEN A **million** DOLLARS SAVED IS NOT ENOUGH TO KEEP PAYING THE BILLS THE AVERAGE AMERICAN HAS.

time value OF MONEY

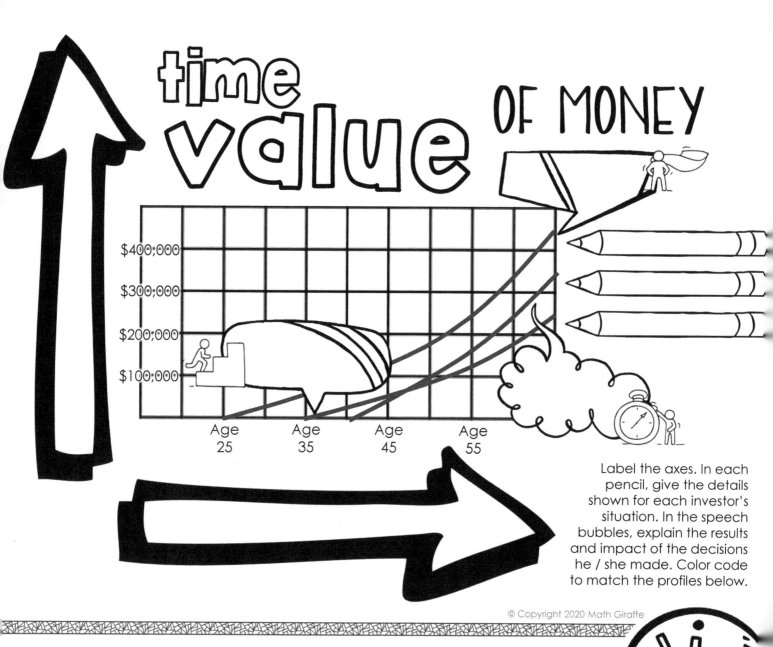

$400,000
$300,000
$200,000
$100,000

Age 25   Age 35   Age 45   Age 55

Label the axes. In each pencil, give the details shown for each investor's situation. In the speech bubbles, explain the results and impact of the decisions he / she made. Color code to match the profiles below.

Use the graph to estimate the value in each account at age 65:

Superstar
EARLY INVESTOR

Lem knows the time value of money. Every small amount he invests early is worth much more later on. His early start on his retirement account at age 25 pays off. He never had to put in more than he could manage easily, but he still ends up with the most value.

playing catch-up
INVESTOR WITH REGRETS

M'Kayla does what many adults do, setting up her investment accounts at age 35. Although the short delay does not seem significant, the fact that she started later than Lem means that she will never achieve the same value in her account.

out of time
DOUBLING DOWN & STILL BEHIND

Roger realizes he is late to the game, and starts investing in his retirement at age 40. He puts in **double** what the others invest, straining his daily income just to make ends meet as he tries to make up for his delay, but he still cannot make up for the lost time to match what Lem did with small, easy contributions.

Each $1 NOW is essentially worth _____ in the future.

WHY?

3
Taxes

$ Create a flow chart
How does a tax system work?

7 Make a bulleted list
Types of Tax Americans Pay

? Doodle some examples
Where does the money go?

Taxes:
the big picture

EXPENSES INCOME

Explain what is meant by
Progressive Tax

a closer look at
Sales Tax

Try calculating sales tax: Find the sales tax and total cost of each purchase in a state that has 8% income tax. Remember to convert the percent to a decimal.

I backpack

4 books

Sales tax rates _____ throughout the country.

$67.99

Books: $4.50 each

To find 8% of $67.99, multiply .08 by $67.99

Depending on where a worker lives, income tax may have to be paid on a _____ level, a _____ level, and even sometimes a local level.

The agency responsible for collecting federal tax and enforcing federal tax laws for the United States is called the:

a closer look at
Income Tax

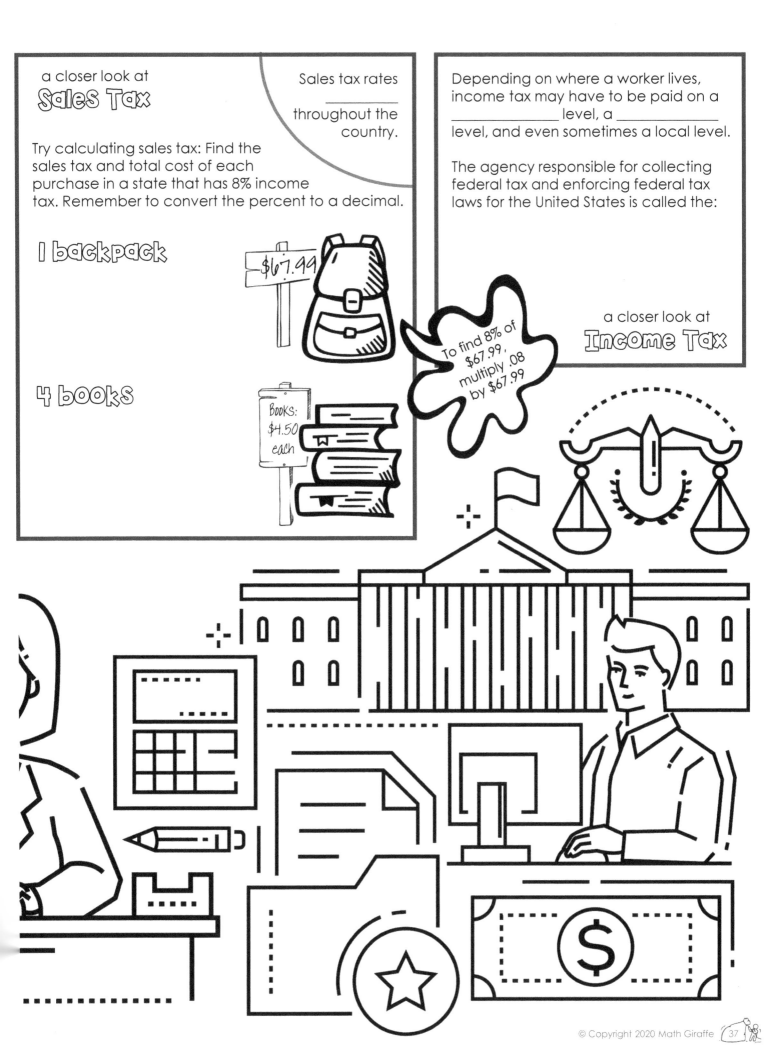

Define each, and label it in the flowchart.

W2:

W4:

1040:

paycheck:

tax withheld:

Color code the words "employee" and "employer" as you fill in the blanks.

Income taxes

_____ fills out a W4

_____ receives a pay stub showing how much was withheld

_____ uses the w4 to determine how much of each paycheck to withhold.

The money that was withheld is sent directly from the

_____ to the government.

At tax time, the _____ sends each worker a W2 that shows the year's income and withholdings.

_____ files his/her taxes using form 1040 and referencing the W2 along with other documents.

You OWE money at tax time if...

You RECEIVE refund money at tax time if...

_____ will either owe more money in taxes or receive a refund.

Filing Your TAXES

withholdings
sometimes need to be adjusted and are based on:

deductions
are amounts that can be _____ from your income before calculating tax. Examples:

dependents

tax brackets & tax tables
Once you have calculated your taxable income and accounted for deductions, you use a chart called a _____ to determine how much tax you should have paid for the year.

Sample Tax Table

Note: The taxpayer is charged in increments, so in this example, the first $20,000 of a married couple's income would be taxed at 10%, then their income from there up to $70,000 would be taxed at 12% and so on. The real tax table you'll reference each year is much more detailed in order to calculate all this for you.

	Taxable Income (Single)	Taxable Income (Married Filing Jointly)
10%	Less than $9,500	Less than $20,000
12%	$9,500 to $35,000	$20,000 to $70,000
16%	$35,001 to $70,000	$70,001 to $100,000
19%	$70,001 to $100,000	$100,001 to $140,000
23%	$100,001 to $145,000	$140,001 to $200,000
27%	$145,001 to $200,000	$200,001 to $300,000
32%	$200,001 to	$300,001 to

What is the top tax rate would a married couple filing jointly (together) have to pay on a taxable income of $152,700?

What is the highest tax rate would a single person have to pay on a taxable income of $41,250?

Explain this difference.

Shade / color ALL the % tax rows that will apply to some portion of the married couple's tax calculation based on the note at the top.

39

What about BUSINESS?

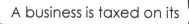

A business is taxed on its _____ rather than on income, like an individual person is taxed.

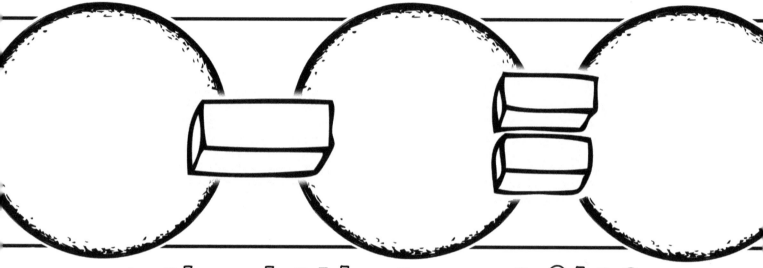

calculating profits

Classify each transaction as REVENUE or EXPENSE and color code.

fees to website developer

print cost for brochures about new offerings

income from in-store customer purchases

money collected from a brand for doing a sponsored post

monthly fee for email marketing services to send emails to customers

credit card transaction fees

electric bills for office

hourly wage paid out to receptionist

expense | color code | revenue

List some ways a business can INCREASE profits.

What are some ways a business can net a LOWER profit in order to pay fewer taxes?

Insurance

group "pool" effect
strategy and probability
risk management
%

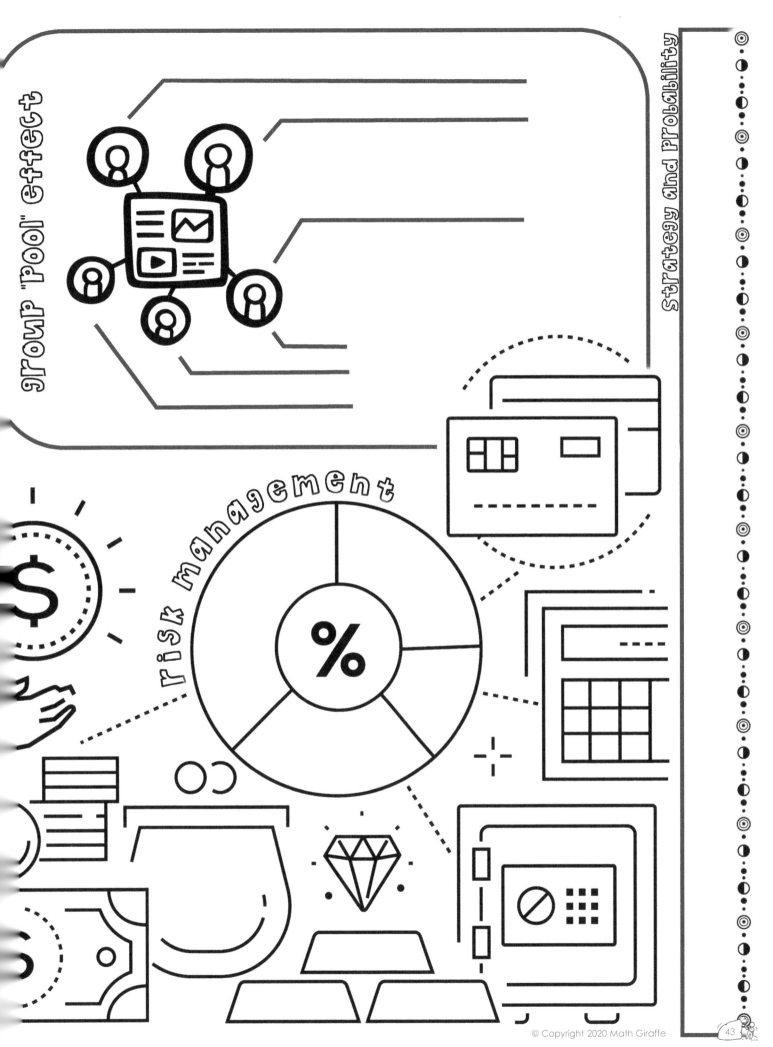

INSURANCE

Policy

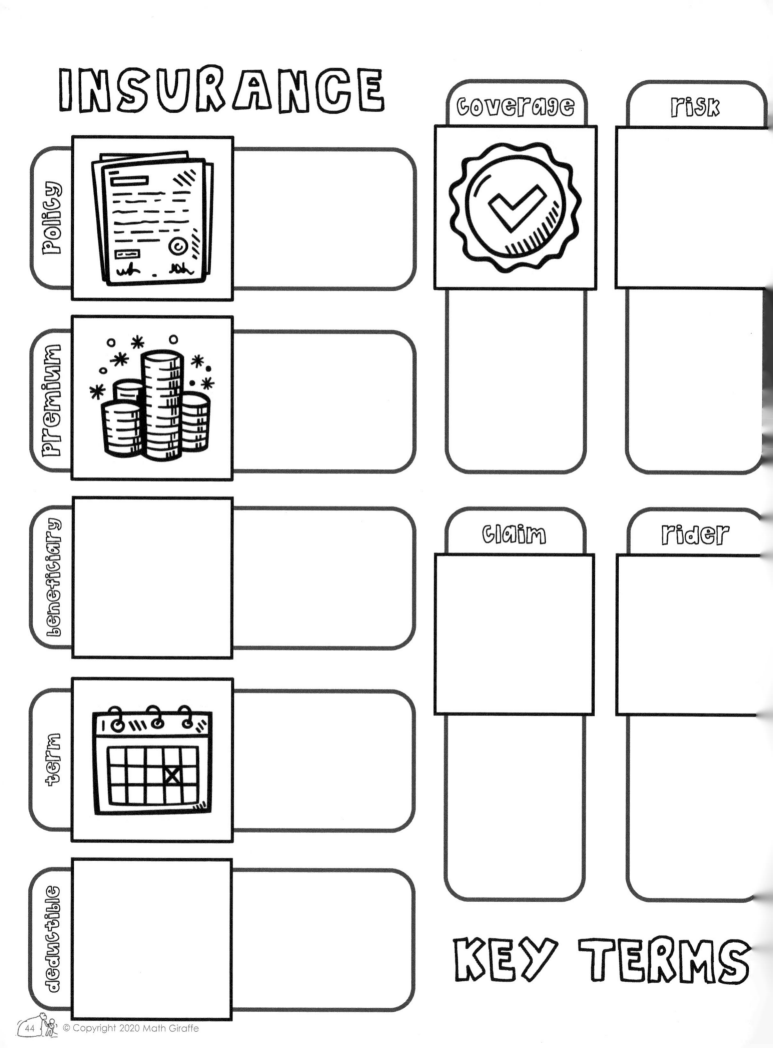

Premium

beneficiary

term

deductible

coverage

risk

claim

rider

KEY TERMS

main types of
INSURANCE

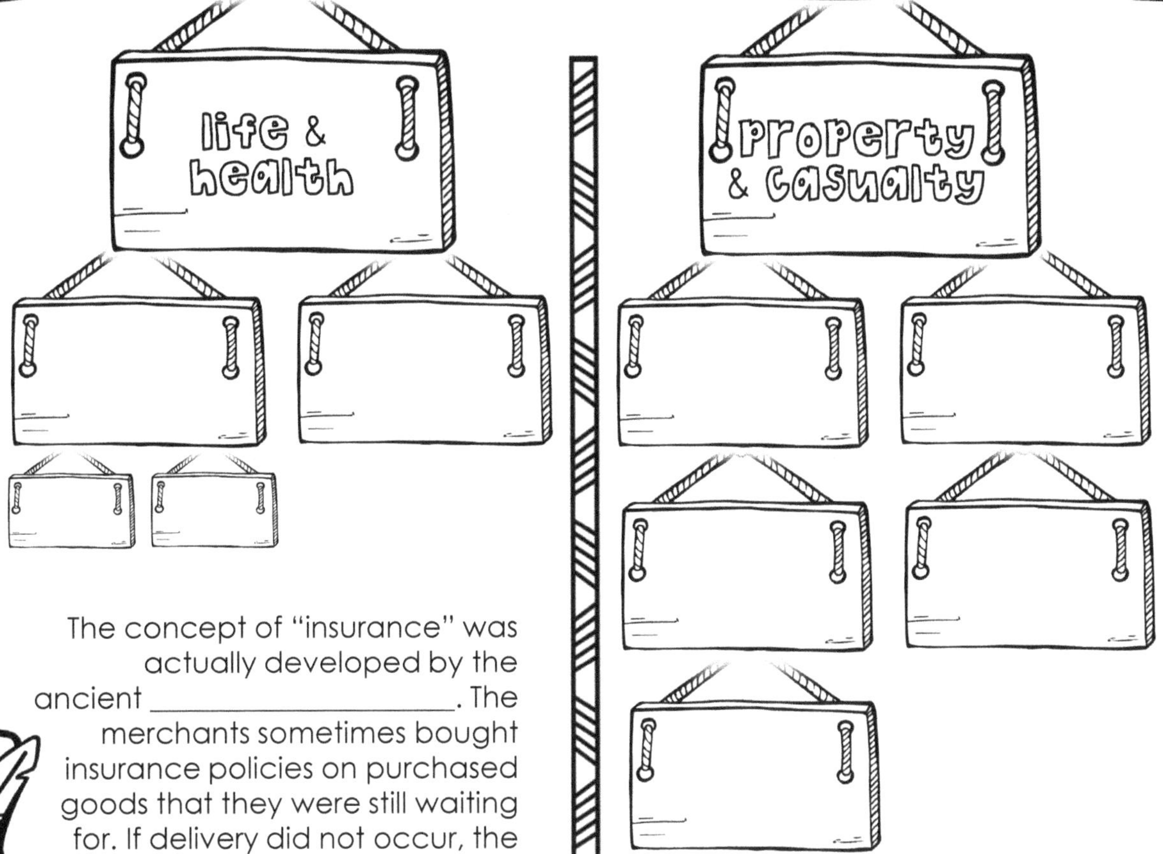

life & health

property & casualty

a little history

The concept of "insurance" was actually developed by the ancient _____. The merchants sometimes bought insurance policies on purchased goods that they were still waiting for. If delivery did not occur, the insurance would give them back the lost money.

Life and health insurance policies protect people from...

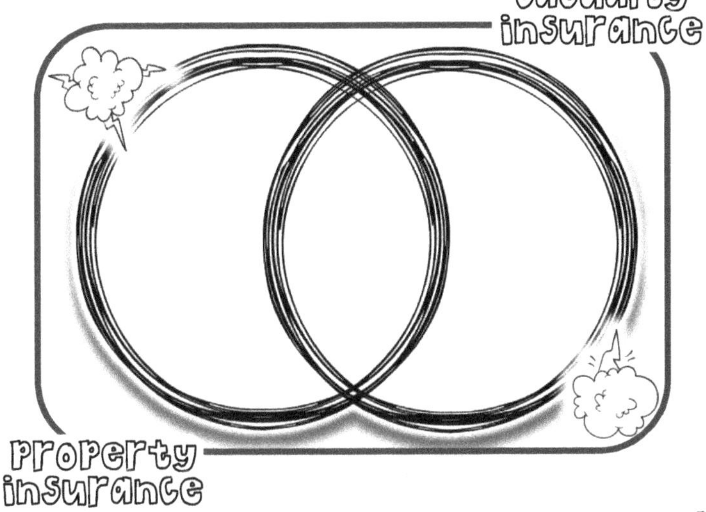

casualty insurance

property insurance

home owners insurance

label what's covered

doodle the danger
What can damage homes?

explain it

What happens if you make a claim

list some factors

That can impact the cost of your home insurance

renters insurance

AUTO
insurance

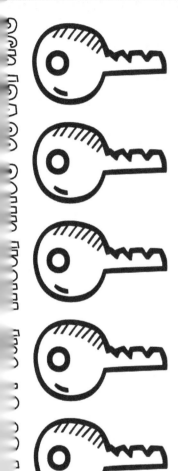

It's the law!

Keeping your
costs low:

liability

property

medical

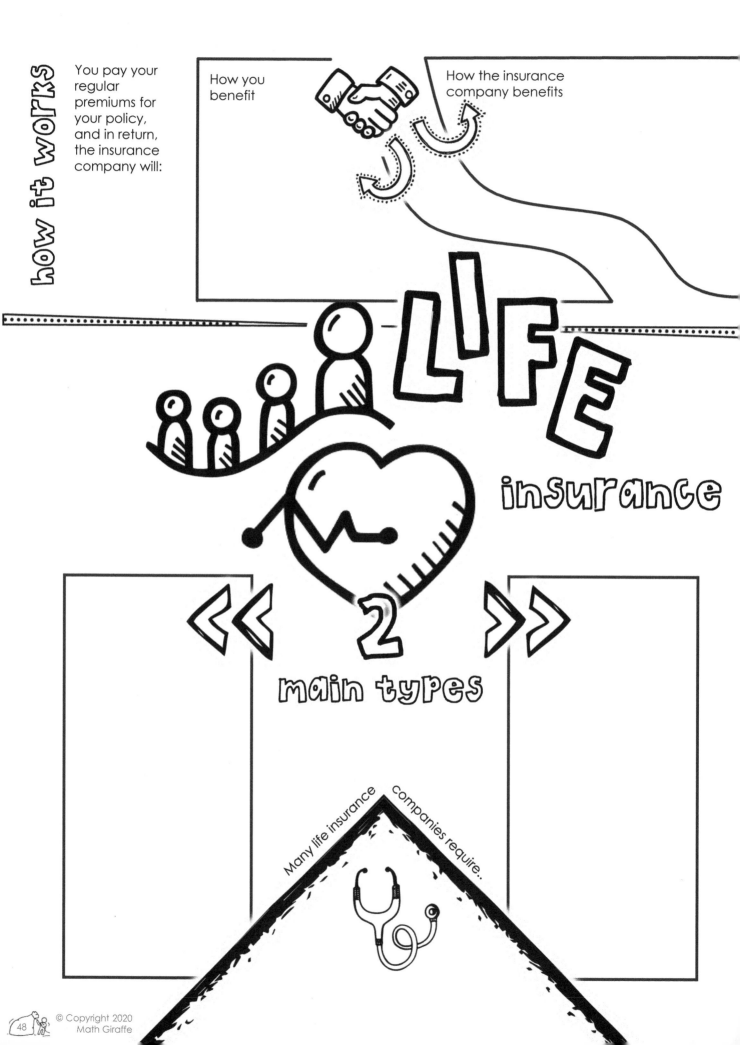

You pay your regular premiums for your policy, and in return, the insurance company will:

How you benefit

How the insurance company benefits

LIFE insurance

<< 2 >>

main types

Many life insurance companies require...

HEALTH  insurance

Medical bills are the ◯ cause of U.S. bankruptcies.

What's covered?

Label 3 types of care. Give examples.

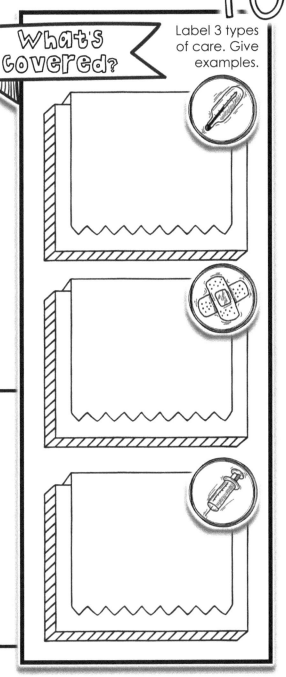

Who needs it?

Costs you may still have
in addition to your premium payments for the plan

amount you'll pay out of pocket before insurance kicks in

the most you'll ever have to pay in a year

amount you pay when you need a specific appointment, health service, or medication

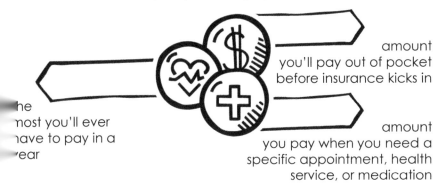

Try it

Geena went in for a doctor appointment, and then they sent her for a diagnostic scan. Her insurance covers the entire doctor visit except for a $10 copay. It also covers 30% of the $350.75 bill for the scan before her deductible is met. (If her deductible for the year *has* been met, the scan will be covered 100%.) She then needs to pick up a prescription that has a total cost of $75.50. With her insurance plan, she only pays a $15 copay for medications. On this particular plan, the copays must be made whether or not the deductible has been met. Find her total cost for this medical situation if she *has* meet her deductible for the year, and her cost if she has not yet.

49

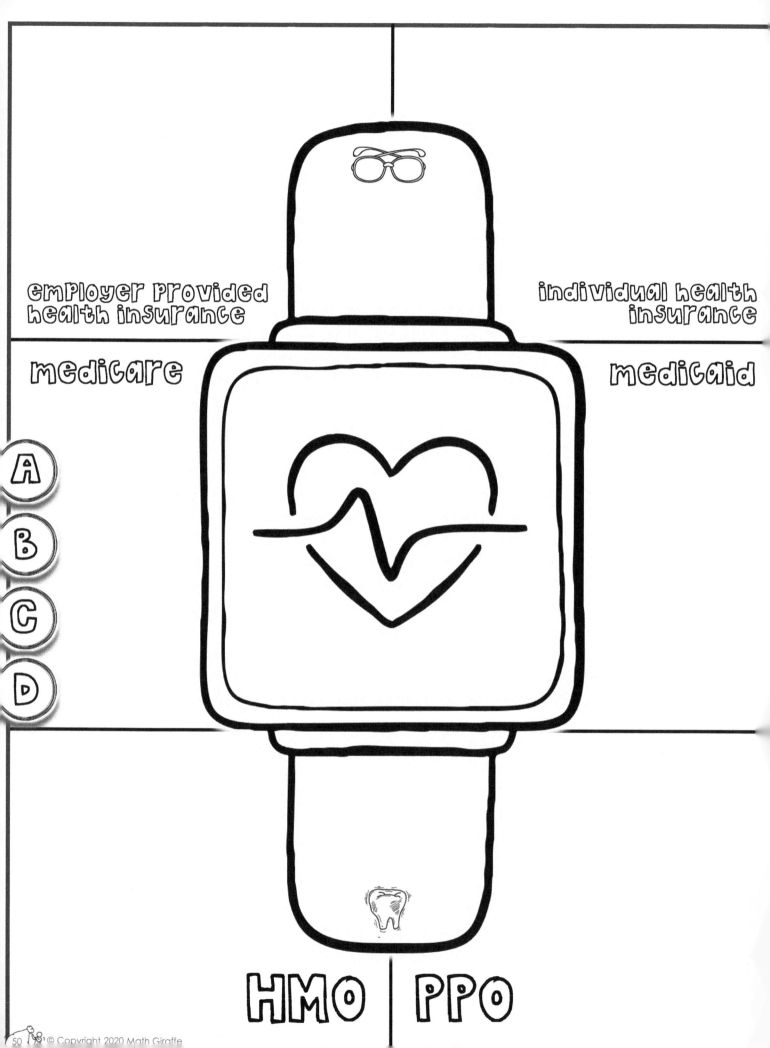

employer provided
health insurance

individual health
insurance

medicare

medicaid

A

B

C

D

HMO | PPO

Some people choose to purchase insurance plans for other thing as well. Assets may be worth insuring if they are either:

SPecialized insurance

Label these types of "other" insurance. Give examples and/or reasons to purchase each.

· ·

Try it

Sergio is purchasing a new phone that he is paying for over the next 2 years on a monthly payment plan. The clerk offers him a protection plan, which is like a small-scale form of insurance for it. He would add $18.50 to each of his monthly payments, and would then get a free replacement, no questions asked, if it breaks within the first three years. What price would the phone have to be before he ends up paying more for the protection plan than the equivalent replacement phone would even be worth?

Do you think it's worth it?

fraud & risk

insurability factors

Imagine you work for the insurance company.

Color risk factors red. Color traits of an individual you can insure with less risk blue.

assess the risk

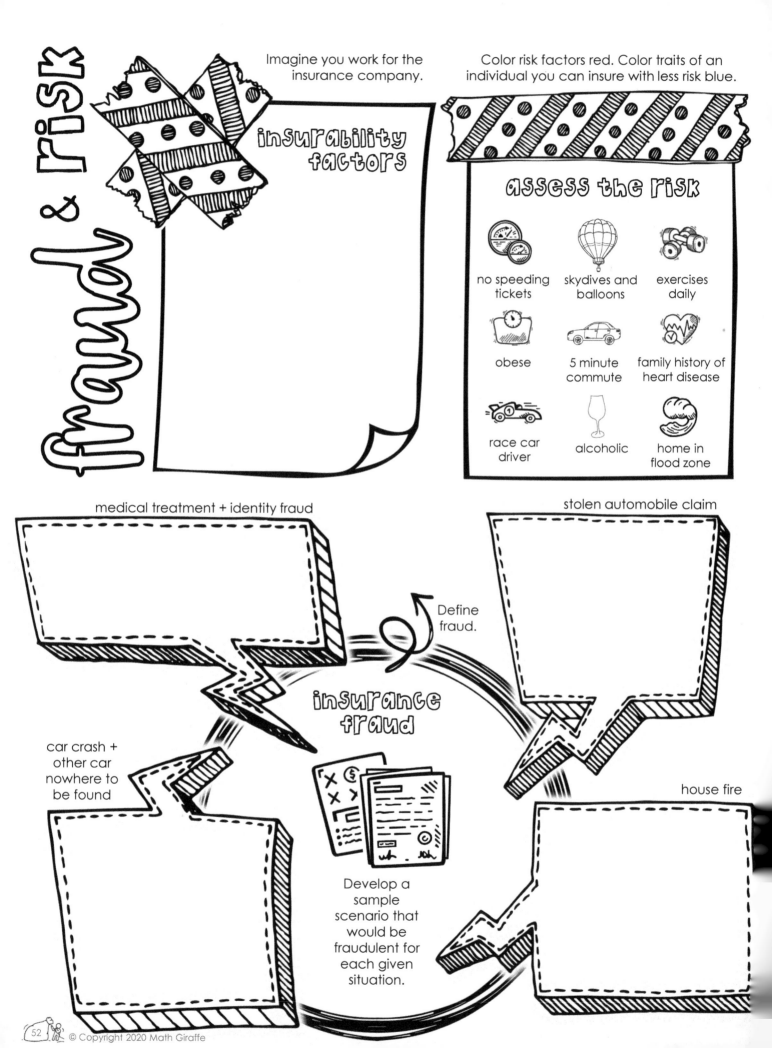

- no speeding tickets
- skydives and balloons
- exercises daily
- obese
- 5 minute commute
- family history of heart disease
- race car driver
- alcoholic
- home in flood zone

medical treatment + identity fraud

stolen automobile claim

Define fraud.

insurance fraud

car crash + other car nowhere to be found

house fire

Develop a sample scenario that would be fraudulent for each given situation.

5 | Mortgages, Loans, & Leases

Many Americans take on debt to pay for their homes, vehicles, and other large expenses.

This strategy allows them to borrow the money to purchase something expensive, like a home, and then slowly pay back the debt owed on that loan in small payments each month.

Here's the catch:

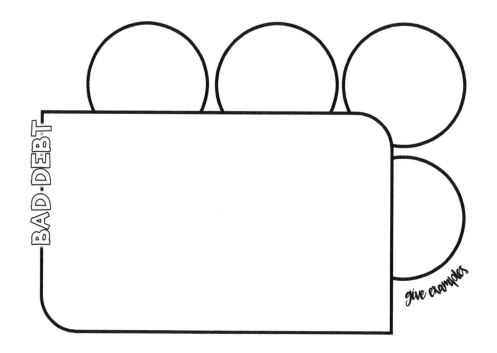

BAD·DEBT

give examples

debt-to-income ratio =

define debt

GOAL:

debt _____

Try it: Calculate the debt-to-income ratio for a person who owes $400 for debts each month and earns $2,000 in gross monthly income.

credit

C _____

C _____

C _____

Why might a person want credit as an option?

Credit Score
➤ Changes over time, depending on
_____

➤ Reflects your credit history and your ability to
_____

➤ Is used by creditors to decide whether or not
_____
_____

How can you start to build credit?

side effects of excessive debt

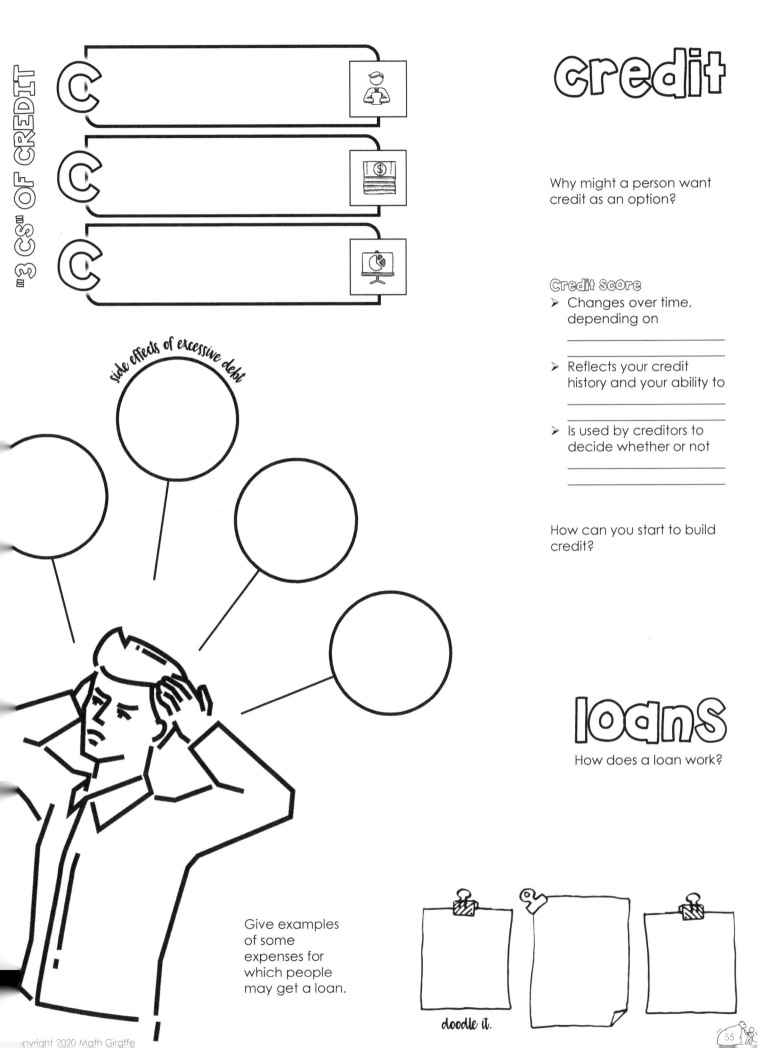

loans

How does a loan work?

Give examples of some expenses for which people may get a loan.

doodle it.

mortgage

Define each key term.

Aiko is purchasing a $215,000 home with a 15% down payment. Her monthly mortgage payment is estimated to be an average of $1,150 for 30 years. This includes the taxes and insurance, as a mortgage payment generally does. How much will she pay in total? Write her down payment in one window, the sum of all her monthly payments in another, and the grand total in the front door.

down payment

interest rate

monthly payment

collateral

fixed rate

adjustable rate

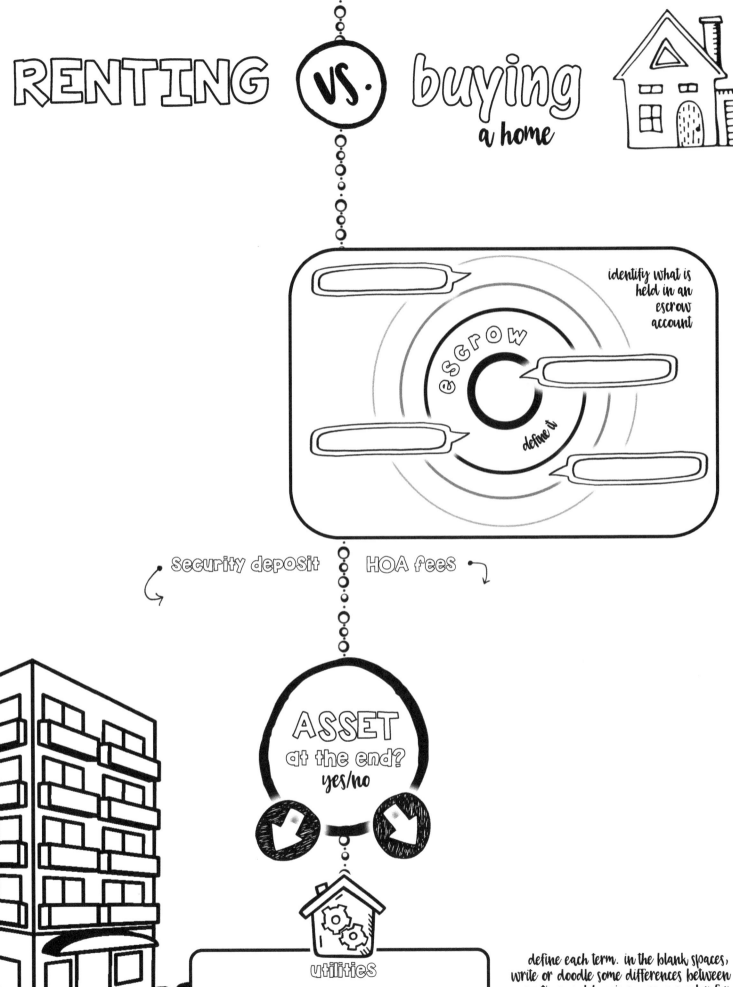

RENTING vs. buying a home

identify what is held in an escrow account

escrow

define it

security deposit · HOA fees

ASSET at the end? yes/no

utilities

define each term. in the blank spaces, write or doodle some differences between renting and buying. use one color for advantages, and one for disadvantages.

LEASING (VS.) buying
a car

title

Lease a Car:
You pay a monthly fee for the vehicle (more like renting).

LIMITATIONS:

ASSET
at the end?
yes/no

Buy a Used Car:
- You will usually pay the entire cost of the vehicle up front.
- You will then have to anticipate

_____

_____ that will vary over time, since the car is older.
- You are the owner of the car and will have it as an

_____, but it is not as valuable as a newer car.

inside the car sections, doodle some dollar signs that represent the different costs of each option. use size or quantity to represent the differences.

Buy a New Car:
- You pay a _____ up front.
- You borrow a loan from the bank. You will then have to pay it back to the bank, a little per month. You will also have to pay them interest. The interest rate will depend on your

_____ (a number that shows lenders how reliable you are at paying back debt). These payments will often last for around 5 or so years.
- You will own the vehicle as an asset when it is paid off at the end of that period of time.

explain "trade in"

VALUE OF ASSETS OVER TIME

sketch and label a graph showing
appreciation of a house

appreciation

in the blank space, give examples of other things that appreciate and depreciate.

·················· define it ··················

depreciation

sketch and label a graph showing
depreciation of a vehicle

College Costs

Some students choose to go to a lower cost college, community college, or only enter a 2-year program instead of a 4+ year program to save money, or if it fits their plans best. Some students go to a 4 year university. The tuition costs can really add up.

Draft up two different career plans that interest you.

Next, investigate the education that is required for each.

Research a sample college tuition schedule to estimate the costs of your plan, or write up the alternative paths that you may take.

In order to pay for college education, many students apply for loans. A parent often has to

_____

and be accountable, since students may not yet have credit built up.

Career

Plan A   Plan B

Student loans:

Identify the two main types of interest accrual.

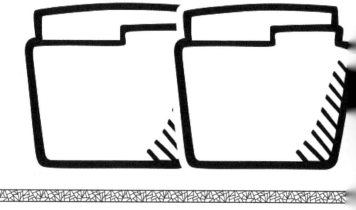

Contracts

Try It

Assume that a student loan that pays for all 4 years of college will cost a total of $65,680 to pay pack. With payments of $325 per month, how long will it take to repay this loan?

6 | Wealth & Worth

WEALTH

- ✗ is not a matter of how much money is **earned**
- ✗ is not a matter of how much money is **spent**
- ✓ actually is about how much money is _____

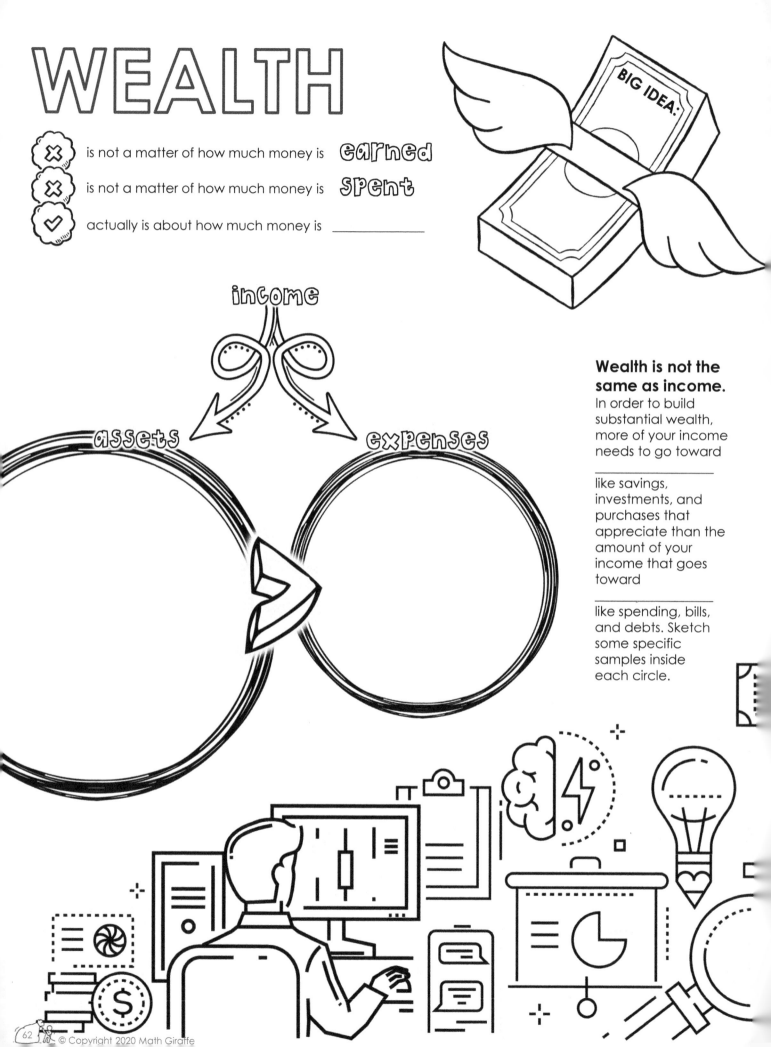

BIG IDEA:

income

assets > expenses

Wealth is not the same as income.
In order to build substantial wealth, more of your income needs to go toward

_____
like savings, investments, and purchases that appreciate than the amount of your income that goes toward

_____
like spending, bills, and debts. Sketch some specific samples inside each circle.

To calculate an individual's worth:

Add up the value of all assets, including things like…

Then subtract the total of any liabilities / debt, such as things like…

NET WORTH

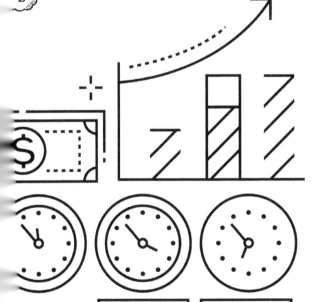

NEW YORK | LONDON | MOSCOW

Explain the differences clearly, including a review of their choices and reasoning for the discrepancies despite having the same yearly salary.

Calculate the net worth for each of these two individuals with the same annual income. Which has done a better job of building wealth with the same level of earning?

JOAN
GENERAL CONTRACTOR
AGE 55
SALARY: $95,000

ASSETS:
Cash in all Accounts: $76,000
401k Retirement Funds: $ 215,000
Home Value: $230,000
Jewelry Collection: $15,000
Vehicle Value: $13,000

DEBTS/LIABILITIES:
Money Owed for Home Mortgage: $64,000
Money Still Owed for Vehicle: $0
Credit Card Debt: $0
Student Loans: $0

ASSETS:
Cash in all Accounts: $12,000
IRA Retirement Funds: $92,000
Home Value: $305,000
Vehicle Value: $55,000
Rental Property: $123,000

DEBTS/LIABILITIES:
Money Owed for Home Mortgages: $320,000
Money Still Owed for Vehicle: $38,000
Credit Card Debt: $6,500
Student Loans: $27,000

RODRIGO
PUBLIC SPEAKER &
ENTREPRENEUR
AGE 48
AVG. YEARLY INCOME:
$95,000

LIFE TIME LINE

Use a color code to mark overlapping ranges on the timeline that represent where you foresee each of these financial "seasons of life" occurring for yourself.

- ☐ Education
- ☐ Part time job
- ☐ Career
- ☐ Side gig
- ☐ Saving
- ☐ Investing
- ☐ Retirement

Phases of life

Your financial goals and priorities will (and should) shift throughout the different phases of life.

Identify the 3 key phases of adult life as far as finance, then label them below the timeline.

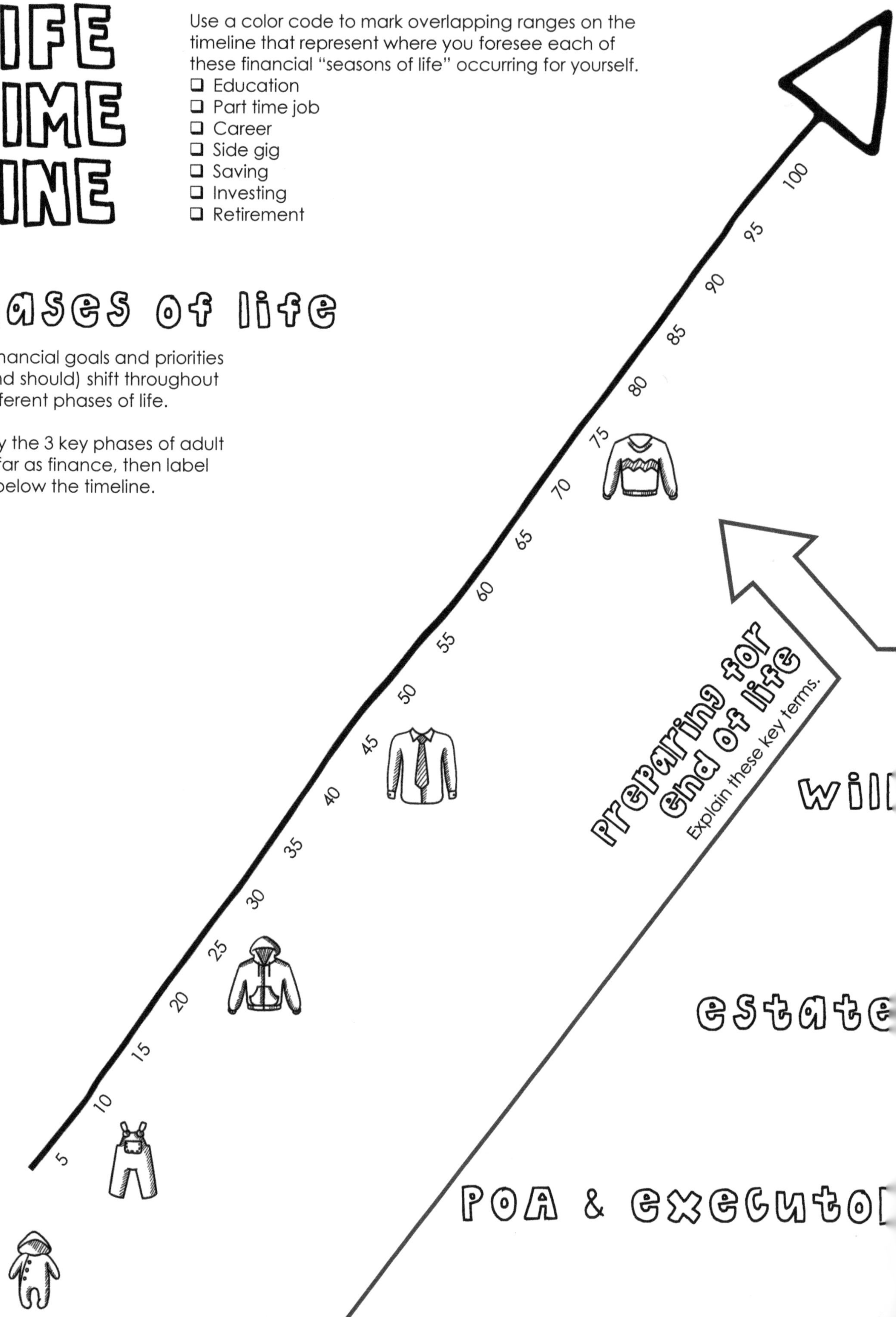

100

95

90

85

80

75

70

65

60

55

50

45

40

35

30

25

20

15

10

5

Preparing for end of life

Explain these key terms.

will

estate

POA & executor

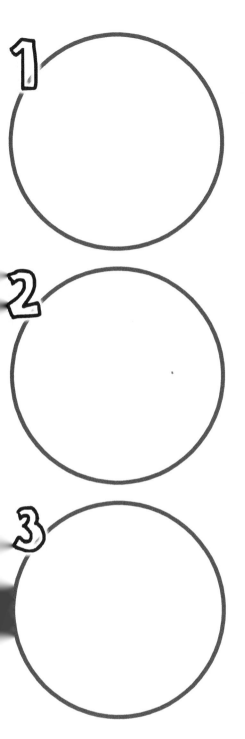

BUILDING WEALTH
is possible for people of all income levels and backgrounds

A survey was done back in 2016 to determine common factors between a wide variety of people who were considered to have a HIGH NET WORTH (They had accumulated a net worth of $3 million or more. Create three colored pie charts inside the circles to represent these three inspiring findings. Sum up what struck you about these facts in the box below with a combination of doodles and text.

1 There is a difference between INCOME and WEALTH. 29% of the millionaires surveyed had less than $200K of income per year! In fact, 55% (more than half) had an income of less than 300k per year, yet still built a net worth of more than three million dollars.

2 77 percent of the millionaires surveyed grew up in either poor or middle class families! That 77% breaks down further into a 19% portion who grew up poor, and a 58% portion who grew up in the middle class.

3 These people with high net worth accumulated about half of their overall wealth as earned income. Another 1/3 of their wealth came from investment returns. Only about 10% of the wealth was inherited.

my most inspiring observation from these facts

Source: 2016 U.S. Trust Wealth and Worth Survey

Key Concept

CASH FLOW ANALYSIS

Some more stats about this group with a net worth of $3 million+ ...

On average, they:

o started **saving** at age **14**

o started **working** at age **15**

o started **giving** to charity and volunteering around age **23**

o began **investing** at age **25**

change the world

WEALTH OFFERS OPPORTUNITIES TO SUPPORT CAUSES YOU ARE PASSIONATE ABOUT

Identify one wealthy person who inspires you. Tell why.

IMPACT

List ways that wealthy people can support a cause in ways that other people sometimes cannot. Out of all the possibilities, highlight the ones that appeal most to you. Dream up some ways to use your future wealth to change the world! Use this motivation to learn more about finance, plan for a smart financial future, and prioritize perfecting your habits.

Highlight the icons that represent your own passions that you support already and you'd prioritize if you were able to build significant wealth. Use the empty spaces to add your own additional causes that you feel will change the world, but require resources, funding, time, and energy.

first steps

TOWARD FINANCIAL STABILITY

Throughout all steps:
>> Continue to increase savings and long-term investments as income grows.
>> Avoid unnecessary _____.

In the thought bubbles, sketch or write some overall priorities that you may have at each early phase of financial planning.

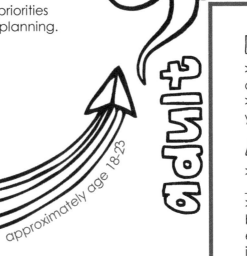

adult

approximately age 18-23

LEARNING:
>> Make decisions about insurance.
>> Learn how to file your own taxes.

ACTION:
>> Start a _____ account.
>> Adjust your budget as your expenses and income change.

teen

approximately age 12-17

LEARNING:
>> Make decisions about continuing education, and attend college if it is in your plans.
>> Investigate housing and vehicle purchasing options in your area and in accordance with the financial outlook of your planned career and salary.

ACTION:
>> Start an _____ fund.
>> Get a part time job.
>> Make a _____.

LEARNING:
>> Get an education, including a high school diploma.
>> Learn the basics of finance as you prepare to become financially independent.
>> Research student loans.

ACTION:
>> Open a savings account if you don't have one yet.
>> Open a _____.
>> Get a student credit card.

Financial goals can be set for a wide range of specific, measurable things. Examples are setting a goal for amount saved in an emergency fund, for net worth, or for certain budgeting ratios to keep spending in proportion with income. In the outer ring of the target, set a minimum acceptable goal for yourself as you are starting out. In the center of the target, set an ultimate goal for building wealth in your life. Once you have a goal, you can take specific steps to get there.

financial goals

HOW?

income streams

How many income streams (on average) does a millionaire have? After you doodle that number inside the ← burst, brainstorm 7 different income streams that would appeal to you. →

Additional Notes

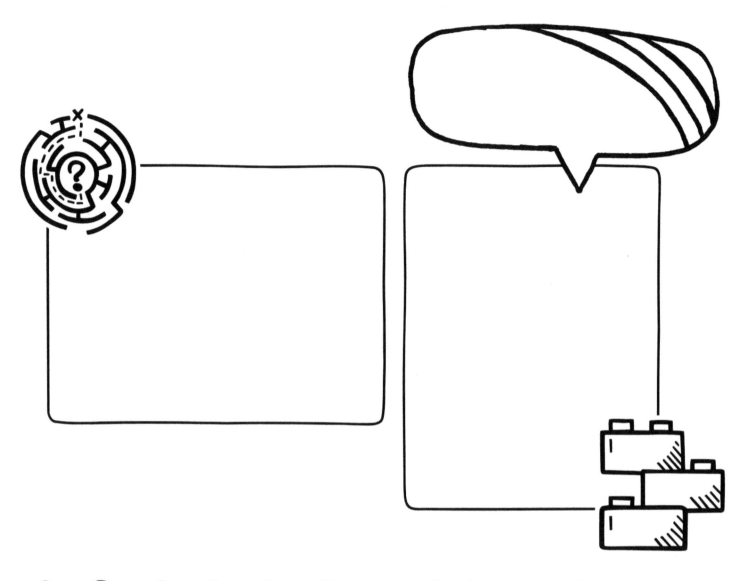

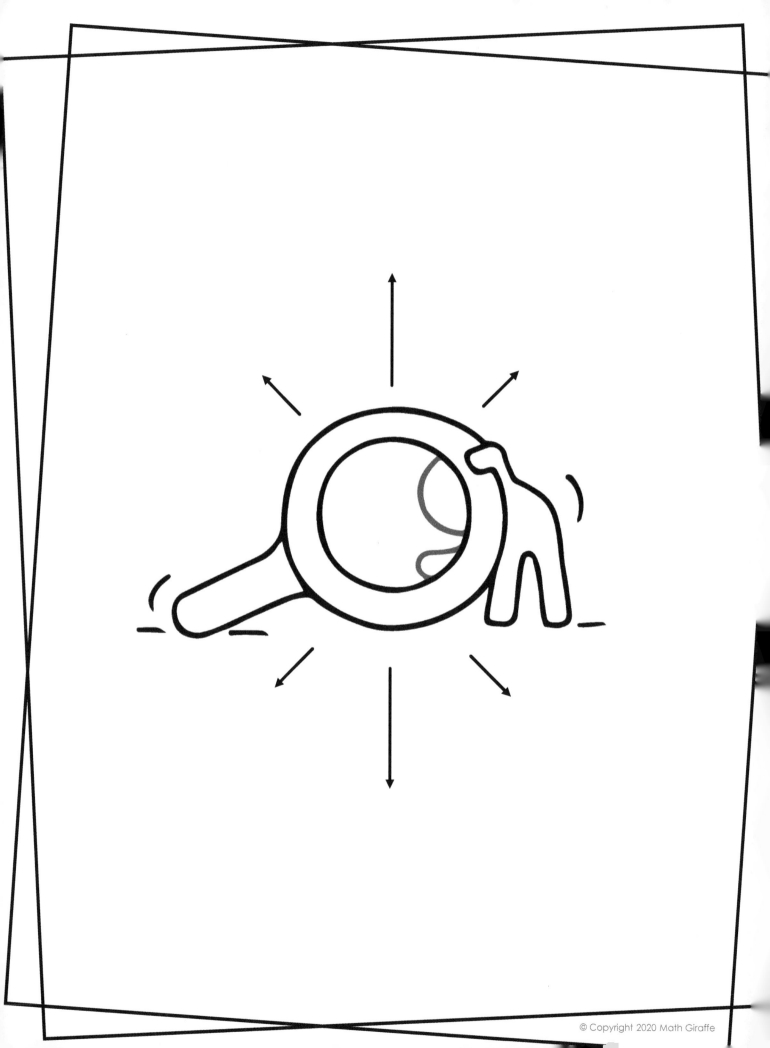

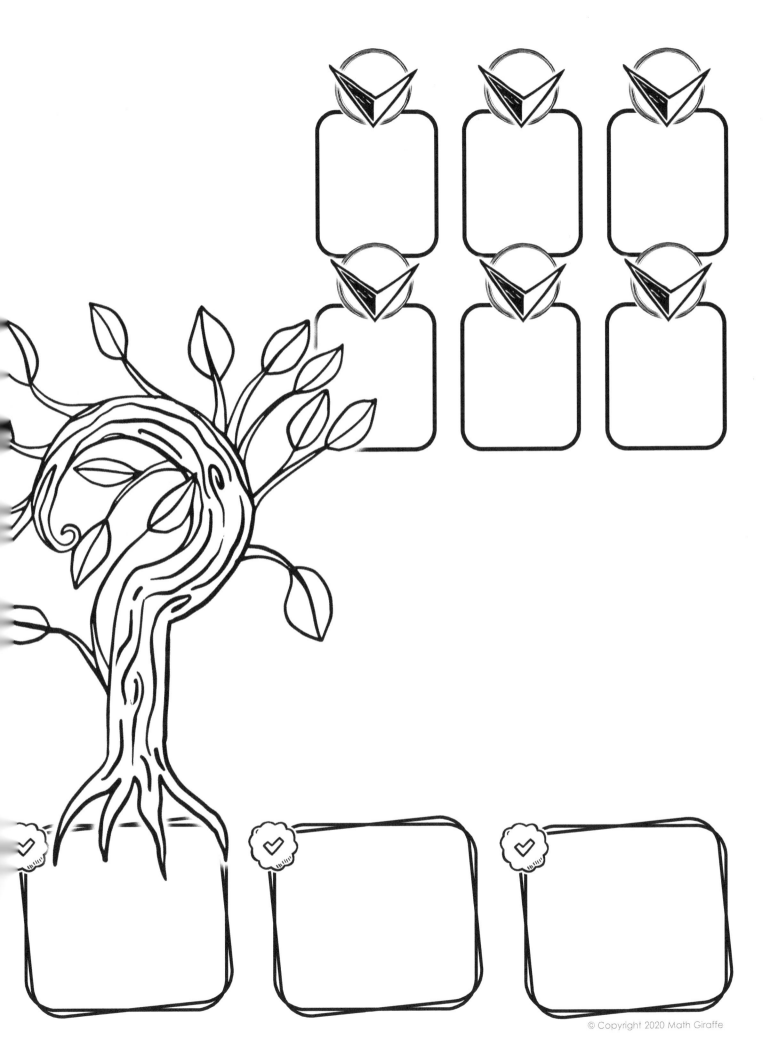

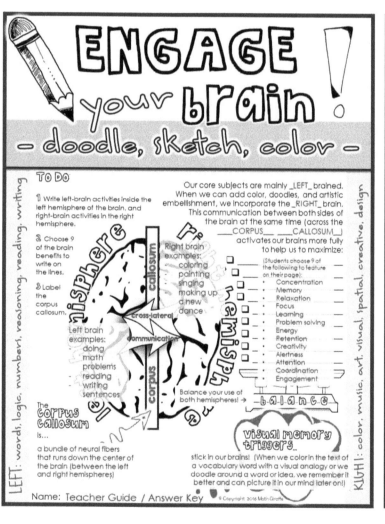

ENGAGE your brain!
- doodle, sketch, color -

TO DO

1 Write left-brain activities inside the left hemisphere of the brain, and right-brain activities in the right hemisphere.

2 Choose 9 of the brain benefits to write on the lines.

3 Label the corpus callosum.

Right brain examples:
coloring
painting
singing
making up a new dance

Left brain examples:
doing math problems
reading
writing sentences

The **corpus callosum** is...
a bundle of neural fibers that runs down the center of the brain (between the left and right hemispheres)

Our core subjects are mainly _LEFT_ brained. When we can add color, doodles, and artistic embellishment, we incorporate the _RIGHT_ brain. This communication between both sides of the brain at the same time (across the ___CORPUS___ ___CALLOSUM___) activates our brains more fully to help us to maximize:

(Students choose 9 of the following to feature on their page):
- Concentration
- Memory
- Relaxation
- Focus
- Learning
- Problem solving
- Energy
- Retention
- Creativity
- Alertness
- Attention
- Coordination
- Engagement

Balance your use of both hemispheres! →

b-a-l-a-n-c-e

visual memory triggers

stick in our brains! (When we color in the text of a vocabulary word with a visual analogy or we doodle around a word or idea, we remember it better and can picture it in our mind later on!)

Name: Teacher Guide / Answer Key
© Copyright 2016 Math Giraffe

LEFT: words, logic, numbers, reasoning, reading, writing

RIGHT: color, music, art, visual, spatial, creative, design

callosum
cross-lateral communication
corpus

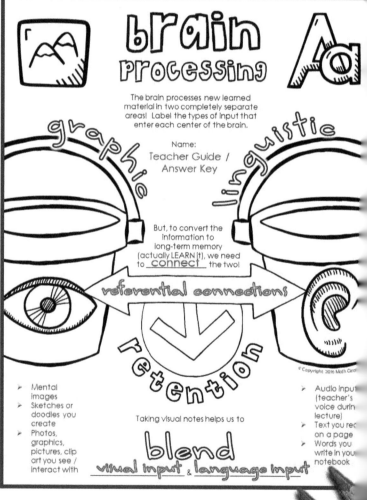

brain processing

The brain processes new learned material in two completely separate areas! Label the types of input that enter each center of the brain.

Name:
Teacher Guide / Answer Key

graphic

linguistic

But, to convert the information to long-term memory (actually LEARN it), we need to __connect__ the two!

referential connections

retention

© Copyright 2016 Math Giraffe

Taking visual notes helps us to

blend
visual input & language input

> Mental images
> Sketches or doodles you create
> Photos, graphics, pictures, clip art you see / interact with

> Audio input (teacher's voice during lecture)
> Text you read on a page
> Words you write in your notebook

MATH GIRAFFE

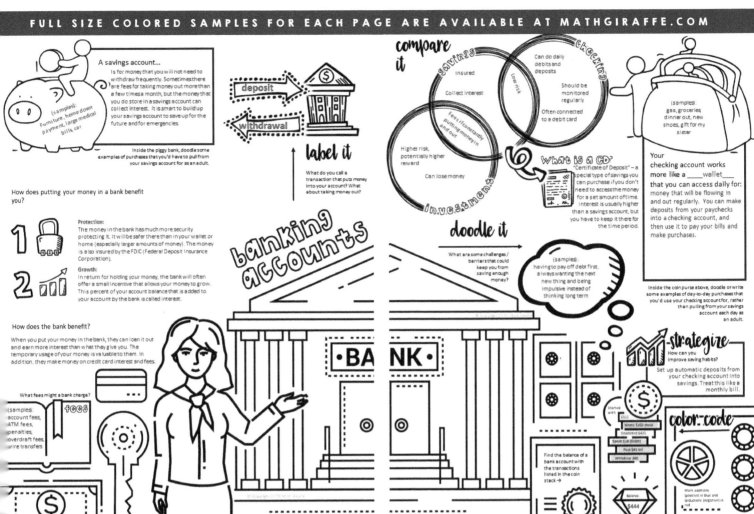

A savings account...
Is for money that you will not need to withdraw frequently. Sometimes there are fees for taking money out more than a few times a month, but the money that you do store in a savings account can collect interest. It is smart to build up your savings account to save up for the future and for emergencies.

(samples): Furniture, home down payment, large medical bills, car

Inside the piggy bank, doodle some examples of purchases that you'd have to pull from your savings account for as an adult.

deposit
withdrawal

label it
What do you call a transaction that puts money into your account? What about taking money out?

How does putting your money in a bank benefit you?

1 Protection:
The money in the bank has much more security protecting it. It will be safer there than in your wallet or home (especially larger amounts of money). The money is also insured by the FDIC (Federal Deposit Insurance Corporation).

2 Growth:
In return for holding your money, the bank will often offer a small incentive that allows your money to grow. This percent of your account balance that is added to your account by the bank is called interest.

How does the bank benefit?

When you put your money in the bank, they can loan it out and earn more interest than what they give you. The temporary usage of your money is valuable to them. In addition, they make money on credit card interest and fees.

What fees might a bank charge?

(samples): account fees, ATM fees, penalties, overdraft fees, wire transfers

fees

banking accounts

•BANK•

compare it
savings / checking / investment

insured
Collect interest
fees! constantly putting money in and out
Higher risk, potentially higher reward
Can lose money

Low risk

Can do daily debits and deposits
Should be monitored regularly
Often connected to a debit card

what is a CD?
"Certificate of Deposit" – a special type of savings you can purchase if you don't need to access the money for a set amount of time. Interest is usually higher than a savings account, but you have to keep it there for the time period.

(samples): gas, groceries, dinner out, new shoes, gift for my sister

Your checking account works more like a ____ wallet ____ that you can access daily for: money that will be flowing in and out regularly. You can make deposits from your paychecks into a checking account, and then use it to pay your bills and make purchases.

doodle it
What are some challenges / barriers that could keep you from saving enough money?

(samples): having to pay off debt first, always wanting the next new thing and being impulsive instead of thinking long term

Inside the coin purse above, doodle or write some examples of day-to-day purchases that you'd use your checking account for, rather than pulling from your savings account each day as an adult.

strategize
How can you improve saving habits?
Set up automatic deposits from your checking account into savings. Treat this like a monthly bill.

Started with: $511
Wrote $450 check
Deposited $425
Spent $16 (Debit)
Paid $45 bill
Withdrew $80

Find the balance of a bank account with the transactions listed in the coin stack →

Balance: $444

color code
Mark additions (positive) in blue and reductions (negative) in red.

DEFINE EACH:

principal
the initial amount invested or deposited

interest rate
the portion (%) of your initial principal deposit that you will get as interest
(This amount is added to your account by the bank.)

interest
amount of money you earn back in addition to your principal (in return for keeping your money there)

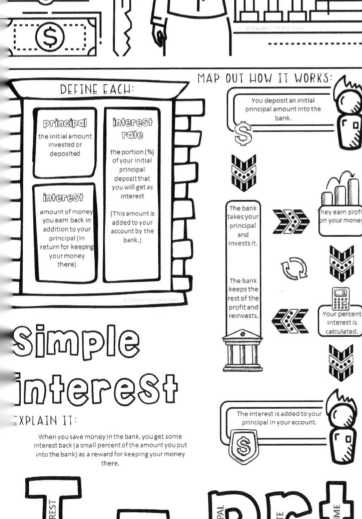

MAP OUT HOW IT WORKS:

You deposit an initial principal amount into the bank.

The bank takes your principal and invests it.

They earn profits on your money.

Your percent interest is calculated.

The bank keeps the rest of the profit and reinvests.

The interest is added to your principal in your account.

Simple interest

EXPLAIN IT:
When you save money in the bank, you get some interest back (a small percent of the amount you put into the bank) as a reward for keeping your money there.

$$I = Prt$$

INTEREST = PRINCIPAL · RATE · TIME
as a decimal   in years

Simple interest
USING THE FORMULA

$$I = Prt$$

INTEREST = PRINCIPAL · RATE · TIME
as a decimal   in years

I DEPOSITED $350 INTO A SAVINGS ACCOUNT WITH 3% INTEREST. HOW MUCH WILL BE IN THE ACCOUNT AFTER 2 YEARS?

I = 350 (0.03) (2)
= 21

*Add that interest amount to the principal, since she asked how much will be in the account (total):

$371

I PLAN TO PUT $500 PER QUARTER INTO AN ACCOUNT WITH 6% INTEREST. HOW MUCH INTEREST WILL I EARN IN THE FIRST QUARTER?

I = 500 (0.06) (0.25)

*We use 0.25 since a quarter is only a fourth of the year.

$7.50

I'M PUTTING ALL $282.50 I EARNED FROM MY JOB INTO MY BANK ACCOUNT. WHAT INTEREST RATE WOULD GET ME TO $300 BY THE END OF THE YEAR?

$17.50 = 282.50 (x)

*17.50 is the amount of interest required to grow the account balance up to $300 (from subtracting $282.50 from the goal of $300)

x ≈ 0.0619

*Convert to a percent for the interest rate:
About 6.2%

SHELTER

hobbies/collection

out to eat/drink

Clothing

NEEDS

WANTS

ADMIT ONE

owed or due for a product or service that's already purchased (IN THE HOLE!) negative

asset owned. valuable that holds its value (or increases in value) over time. examples: land, houses, some equipment

A **debit card** (usually issued by your bank to go w. a checking acct.) that takes $ right from your acct. to buy things

credit card the payment is made for you, but you then owe it back to the credit card company (with interest) if you wait to pay)

cash back When you pay in a debit card, you can sometimes add to the bill + get it back as change. (Get cash without an ATM)

Patience Pays! Any time you can save up the $ BEFORE making a purchase, you'll pay less than if you pay off credit slowly

DELAYED GRATIFICATION

Many people don't realize how long a debt will follow them. It gets harder and harder to dig out as interest accumulates. Debt grows automatically over time if you don't pay it off quickly!

managing spending

EXTRAS TO BUDGET FOR:

Before planning to budget $ for certain purchases, be aware of these additions. These expenses may be added on top of the cost of goods / services.

extra costs added on ➡

tip When you receive service from a waiter, delivery person, or driver, you often give a % tip.

sales tax most states collect a %.

fees Some purchases incur additional fixed amounts

EXAMPLE TIPS/FEES
• shipping
• delivery fee
• installation
• tip hotel staff

© Copyright 2020 Math Giraffe

label it

Use hand lettering to place each of these terms somewhere in the correct area of the flowchart and explain.

- Withholdings
- Tips
- Extra / Entertainment
- Paycheck
- Work
- Food, Medical, & Other Needs
- Savings
- Gross Pay
- Home expenses and bills
- Net Pay
- Benefits

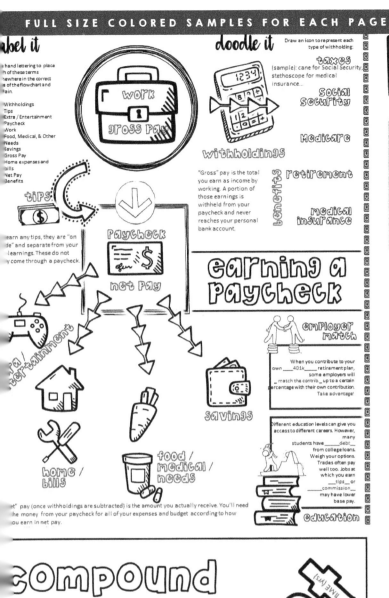

tips

If you earn any tips, they are "on the side" and separate from your true earnings. These do not usually come through a paycheck.

paycheck / net pay

Work / gross pay

doodle it

Draw an icon to represent each type of withholding:

taxes
(sample: cane for Social Security, stethoscope for medical insurance...)

social security

Medicare

withholdings

"Gross" pay is the total you earn as income by working. A portion of those earnings is withheld from your paycheck and never reaches your personal bank account.

benefits / retirement

medical insurance

earning a paycheck

employer match

When you contribute to your own ____401k____ retirement plan, some employers will __match__ the contrib. up to a certain percentage with their own contribution. Take advantage!

savings

Different education levels can give you access to different careers. However, many students have ____debt____ from college loans. Weigh your options. Trades often pay well too. Jobs at which you earn ____tips____ or ____commission____ may have lower base pay.

education

extra / entertainment

home / bills

food / medical / needs

"Net" pay (once withholdings are subtracted) is the amount you actually receive. You'll need the money from your paycheck for all of your expenses and budget according to how you earn in net pay.

---

reading a paycheck

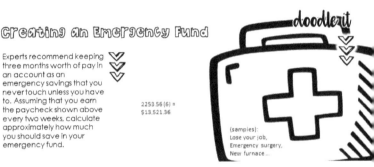

Pay to the order of: _____

1519

Two thousand two hundred fifty-three and 56/100 dollars   **$2,253.56**

Pay Period: Dec. 1 through Dec. 14, 2015	**Total Earnings**	**Withholdings**	
pretend paycheck, math purposes only	**$3121.14**	Federal Tax:	$513.25
		Social Security:	$256.19
		Medicare:	$98.14

Assume that the paycheck shown here is the first one you receive for a new career with consistent income. To kick off a good savings habit with your new income, you plan to deposit one paycheck (half of your first month's income, since each month you earn two paychecks) into an account with simple interest. The interest rate is 2.25%. Calculate the total amount that you would have in the account after 10 years.

$$i = 2253.56 \,(.0225)(10) = \$507.05 \text{ in interest}$$

$$\$2760.61 \text{ total}$$

try it

Compare the gross pay and net pay on this simplified sample paycheck. Find the total percent of your earnings that were withheld from your check. What percent of your gross pay do you actually receive?

Approx. 27.8% is withheld

Receive approx. 72.2% of gross pay

In the box, write or draw cases that may require you to access your emergency fund.

Creating an Emergency Fund

Experts recommend keeping three months worth of pay in an account as an emergency savings that you never touch unless you have to. Assuming that you earn the paycheck shown above every two weeks, calculate approximately how much you should save in your emergency fund.

$$2253.56 \,(6) = \$13,521.36$$

doodle it

(samples):
Lose your job,
Emergency surgery,
New furnace ...

---

compound interest

NAME: Answer Key / Teacher Guide

$$A = P\left(1 + \frac{r}{n}\right)^{nt}$$

Interest rate goes into the formula in decimal format.

TIME (yrs)

# of times compounded (or # of periods)

RATE

PRINCIPAL

AMOUNT / BALANCE

SIMPLE VS. COMPOUND INTEREST

What's the difference?

Instead of only making interest on your principal, with compound interest you make interest on your principal AND the interest accumulated. The interest is compounded multiple times and keeps being added back into the balance.

What's included in the balance?

- Principal
- Interest

TRY IT

Find the balance after 6 years on an account with 3.5% interest with a $4,000 principal compounded monthly.

$$A = 4000\left(1 + \frac{0.035}{12}\right)^{12(6)}$$

$$\$4993.20$$

(You may want to allow calculators here, but be sure to remind students to be cautious about the order of operations.)

How many times per year (n)?

MONTHLY	12
QUARTERLY	4
SEMIANNUALLY	2

SIMPLE VS. COMPOUND INTEREST: SKETCH IT

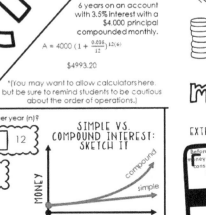

MONEY / TIME — compound / simple

NEEDS	WANTS
(Write or doodle expenses that fall into the "needs" category for budgeting)	(Write or doodle expenses that fall into the "wants" category for budgeting)

When you can save up BEFORE making a purchase, you'll always pay less than if you buy it on credit and pay it off afterward. Be patient!

DELAYED GRATIFICATION

Many people do not realize how long a debt will follow them. It gets harder and harder to get out, since debt automatically grows over time.

managing spending

EXTRAS TO BUDGET FOR:

These expenses may be added on top of the cost of goods / services.

tip — Before planning to spend / budget money for certain goods and services, consider what extra costs will be added to the amount. When you receive service from a waitress, delivery person, or driver, it's customary to give a percent of the cost as a tip.

sales tax — Most states charge a percent of a purchase of goods as tax.

fees — Some purchases will have additional fees (set dollar amount that are added to your bill) as well.

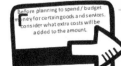

debt
Money that is owed, or due for a service or product already purchased (IN THE HOLE, figuratively speaking – negative money!)

asset
Owned valuables, that will either hold their value or appreciate (grow) in monetary worth, like land or houses tend to do over time

debit card
When processed, removes money directly from the account

credit card
The payment is made for you, but you owe it back to the card company (with interest if not paid off right away)

cash back
When you pay with a debit card and select this, the $ is added to your bill, but you receive it as change (avoids finding an ATM & paying ATM fees)

EXAMPLE TIPS/FEES
(samples):
Shipping & handling
Delivery/installation fee
Tipping hotel staff
Textbook fee (college)

Simple Interest:

$$I = p \cdot r \cdot t$$

where I is the interest accumulated, p is the principal (starting) amount, r is the interest rate in decimal form, and t is time in years. The interest you have earned is then added to the principal at the end of the year.

Compound Interest:

$$A = P\left(1 + \frac{r}{n}\right)^{nt}$$

P is the principal (initial value), r is the interest rate in decimal form, n is the number of times per year that the interest is compounded, and t is the number of years.

interest is added on top of $ already in there

accelerating the increases over time

Calculating interest

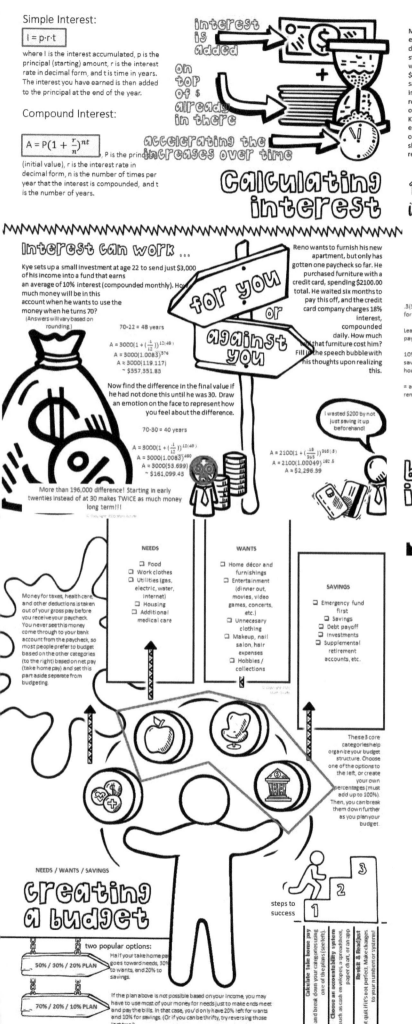

interest can work ...

Kye sets up a small investment at age 22 to send just $3,000 of his income into a fund that earns an average of 10% interest (compounded monthly). How much money will be in this account when he wants to use the money when he turns 70?
(Answers will vary based on rounding.)

for you or **against you**

70-22 = 48 years

$A = 3000(1 + (\frac{1}{12}))^{12(48)}$
$A = 3000(1.0083)^{576}$
$A = 3000(119.117)$
$\approx $357,351.83$

Now find the difference in the final value if he had not done this until he was 30. Draw an emotion on the face to represent how you feel about the difference.

70-30 = 40 years

$A = 3000(1 + (\frac{1}{12}))^{12(40)}$
$A = 3000(1.0083)^{480}$
$A = 3000(53.699)$
$\approx $161,099.45$

More than 196,000 difference! Starting in early twenties instead of at 30 makes TWICE as much money long term!!!

Reno wants to furnish his new apartment, but only has gotten one paycheck so far. He purchased furniture with a credit card, spending $2100.00 total. He waited six months to pay this off, and the credit card company charges 18% interest, compounded daily. How much will that furniture cost him? Fill in the speech bubble with his thoughts upon realizing this.

I wasted $200 by not just saving it up beforehand!

$A = 2100(1 + (\frac{18}{365}))^{365(.5)}$
$A = 2100(1.00049)^{182.5}$
$A \approx $2,296.39$

Myah went to trade school and earned a small salary as an apprentice during her education. Now, she is starting her career as an electrician without any debt. She will earn $55,000 per year as her starting salary. She assumes that 30% of her income will go toward taxes, retirement, etc. She then will put 10% of her take-home pay into savings. Knowing that she will have other expenses, she plans to spend only 25% of her net pay on housing. How much should she budget for her rent/mortgage?

2 compare it

Although Jen's salary is a little higher, and the housing cost is a smaller % of her budget, she has a lot of college debt. She will have less for wants/spending until it's paid off.

Myah has been earning money longer and doesn't have the college loan debt. However, her salary is a bit lower (at least for now), so she has to budget a higher % of her income for the rent.

1 calculate it

.3(55000) = 16,500 deducted for taxes, retirement, etc.

Leaves 38,500 as take home pay

10% of that is $3850 toward savings, and 25% is $9,625 as housing budget for the year

= about $800 per month for rent / mortgage

Jen accumulated $45,000 in college debt. Now, she is starting her career in IT support. She will earn $65,000 per year as her starting salary. She assumes that 30% of her income will go toward taxes, retirement, etc. She then will put 10% of her take-home pay into savings. What percent of her net pay would she have to budget for housing to be Myah's roommate, splitting the rent/mortgage equally?

.3(65000) = 19,500 deducted for taxes, retirement, etc.

Leaves 45,500 as take home pay

10% of that is $4550 toward savings

She'd need to spend $800 a month (or about $9600 per year) for rent / mortgage to match Myah's contribution to the housing.

What portion of her take home pay is that?:
9600 = x% (45500)
x ≈ 21% of her take home pay

Food budget is often around 11% of a person's total take home pay. Find Jen's food budget and Myah's food budget.

.11(38500) = $4,235 per year ($353 month) for Myah

.11(45500) = $5,005 per year ($417 month) for Jen

balancing income and expenses

NEEDS
- ☐ Food
- ☐ Work clothes
- ☐ Utilities (gas, electric, water, internet)
- ☐ Housing
- ☐ Additional medical care

WANTS
- ☐ Home décor and furnishings
- ☐ Entertainment (dinner out, movies, video games, concerts, etc.)
- ☐ Unnecessary clothing
- ☐ Makeup, nail salon, hair expenses
- ☐ Hobbies / collections

SAVINGS
- ☐ Emergency fund first
- ☐ Savings
- ☐ Debt payoff
- ☐ Investments
- ☐ Supplemental retirement accounts, etc.

Money for taxes, health care, and other deductions is taken out of your gross pay before you receive your paycheck. You never see this money come through to your bank account from the paycheck, so most people prefer to budget based on the other categories (to the right) based on net pay (take home pay) and set this part aside separate from budgeting.

These 3 core categories help organize your budget structure. Choose one of the options to the left, or create your own percentages (must add up to 100%). Then, you can break them down further as you plan your budget.

NEEDS / WANTS / SAVINGS

creating a budget

two popular options:

50% / 30% / 20% PLAN
Half your take home pay goes toward needs, 30% to wants, and 20% to savings.

70% / 20% / 10% PLAN
If the plan above is not possible based on your income, you may have to use most of your money for needs just to make ends meet and pay the bills. In that case, you'd have 20% left for wants and 10% for savings. (Or if you can be thrifty, try reversing those last two!)

Calculate take home pay and break down your categories using one of the plans (see left).

Choose an accountability system such as a spreadsheet, paper chart, or an app.

Revisit & Readjust if it's not quite right. Make changes to your numbers or systems!

steps to success
1 2 3

building a budget

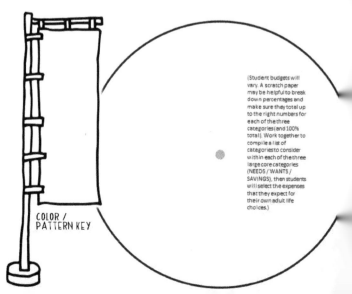

First, form three large segments (needs, wants, and savings). Use light color shading to identify each, and label each with a percent. (Make sure it adds up to 100% to represent total take-home pay!)

Then, break each of your three categories into smaller sub-segments. You decide what smaller percent each should [...] up (food, bills, gas, entertainment, etc.). Within the correct color group, add pattern to differentiate these segments and label each in the key beside the graph. Take your tim[...] Don't miss anything that is important to you! Research costs and verify that your budgeting plan is practical. Test [...] life amounts of take-home pay to see if your dollar amounts would actually work based on the percentages you ch[...]

COLOR / PATTERN KEY

(Student budgets will vary. A scratch paper may be helpful to break down percentages and make sure they total up to the right numbers for each of the three categories (and 100% total). Work together to compile a list of categories to consider within each of the three large core categories (NEEDS / WANTS / SAVINGS), then students will select the expenses that they expect for their own adult life choices.)

investment
(label and explain)

timeline — The length of time your money is invested makes a big difference in the growth. For a long-term investment, you'll have the time value of money on your side, and any dips in the market will iron out so your growth trends upward. For an investment of only a few years, you'll need to plan differently and account for market volatility. A different type of investment may be wiser for each different time span.

goals — Your goals for the money invested also must be taken into account. If you are planning for retirement, you'll set up your investment differently than if you are investing your down payment for a home for 5 years to help it grow before you make your purchase at that point.

percent return — Different types of investment have different percent return. Some may have the potential for high growth (reward) but also have high risk (possibility to lose the money you invested). The average annual return (gain) is a key factor to keep in mind when choosing an investment.

risk — Unlike a savings account, an investment comes with risk. You could lose your money. In exchange for the potential for more growth than just the savings interest would earn, an investor must accept that risk. "high risk, high reward"

growth — An investment has the potential to earn exponential growth (a curve that grows more rapidly than linear growth) – see graphs. However, the graphs in fact will look more like this over time because of the shifts in the market:

Investment values will dip periodically, but over long periods of time it still generally trends upward.

KEY FACTORS TO UNDERSTAND:
- ☐ TIMELINE
- ☐ GOALS
- ☐ % RETURN
- ☐ RISK
- ☐ GROWTH

Investment: The process of putting your money to work by directly or indirectly buying assets and holding onto them as their value grows.

Buying stocks, owning real estate, and investing in my retirement account are like watering a money tree. I'll be able to pick off the leaves and use the fruits of the investment later on.

The average annual return for savings: 0-2%
The average annual return for investment: 6-10%

Lay aside money now in exchange for MORE money in the future.

DOODLE IT: RISK & REWARD

Comparing growth
Students can use an online calculator to approximate $ at a few points in time, then connect to form a curve.

Compare keeping $1000 in savings gaining 2% interest with investing $1000 in a fund averaging 8% annual return. Label axes and plot year 40.

GRAPH IT
$10,000 / $5,000 — ~$2,000 — TIME 10 20 30 40

EXPLAIN IT — The low annual rate of return keeps this fund slowly growing, but even after 40 years, the $1000 is only worth a little more than $2,000.

GRAPH IT
$20,000 / $15,000 / $10,000 / $5,000 — ~$20,000 — TIME 10 20 30 40

(Note the HUGE DIFFERENCE!)

EXPLAIN IT — The high annual rate of return compounds to make the growth rate keep increasing. The fund grows faster and faster, and the original $1000 is worth more than $20,000 after 40 years!

---

stocks
are small shares of ownership in a company that can be purchased (The investor earns partial distributions based on the success and profits of the business.)

bonds
allow a large entity (like the government or a large corporation) to hold and use your money for a set period of time. Bonds can be bought or sold. (Essentially, the investor is lending their money as a loan. The government or other entity then pays it back with interest for the use of the funds.)

Example: 10 year U.S. Treasury Note

index funds — are a passive investment option that contain a full range of stocks (holding all of the stocks within an entire index.) They are therefore diversified to remain stable over long periods of time and track the performance of a financial market's index. Many people will invest in these funds, similar to a mutual fund.

are collections of professional investments that are managed by experts. (Many people together invest in a strategically balanced portfolio of stocks, bonds, and other assets.)

What about cash? — It's wise to maintain some cash, just because it is the least risky way to keep money. Its value will not drop drastically like the value of a stock sometimes can. Most investors keep a small percent of their wealth as cash, to reduce risk and have some funds easily accessible.

Tangible assets, like land, real estate, or gold also can be investments, because their value naturally increases over time.

Color code each segment, draw icons or illustrations to represent each type of investment, and explain.

(Icons and drawings will vary to represent how each student will help remember each type of investment.)

diversification — A healthy collection of investments will have some high risk, some medium risk, and some low risk holdings. The goal is to ensure growth, but minimize the risk as much as possible by balancing it out.

types of investment

THE STOCK MARKET
Shares (small pieces of ownership) in different companies are bought and sold. Investors buy and sell stocks and can earn profits either by timing their purchases and sales strategically, or by holding onto their shares for a long period of time. They can also potentially lose money on these transactions, though.

COMPANIES — To get money, a business will sell off pieces of ownership (partial shares in the company) to investors. **Raise money** by giving up fractional ownership of the business

STOCK: SHARE — The value of the stock will rise and fall with the success/ failure of the business. "Stock" is a small percentage of ownership in the company, giving the holder a cut of the profits.

Buying and selling of these shares happens within the stock market.

INVESTORS — Investors will strategically buy and sell their shares at the right time, trying to predict when the values will rise and fall. **Buy and sell stocks** to try to earn a profit (sometimes through a broker)

STOCK EXCHANGE — There is a risk that a stock's value may drop suddenly. Prices within the market rise and fall. When a stockholder can sell a share for more money than he/she bought it for (based on timing as its value rises and falls), he/she can make money.

The goal is to "buy low, sell high." (Purchase when the price is low but likely to rise, and then sell it when you expect that it has gone as high as it will go and is about to drop.)

Investors are continually buying and selling, although some hold stocks for very long periods of time.

CAPITAL LOSS — when you sell the stock, its price is lower than what you paid for it (OOPS)

CAPITAL GAINS (profit) — when you sell the stock, its price is higher than what you paid for it (YAY)

SELLING STOCK

HOW RETIREMENT ACCOUNTS WORK:

You contribute a portion of your monthly earnings, and it gets invested. Often, the money goes into mutual funds, which are collections of stocks. This money will usually grow so you can use it as income when you an older adult and are no longer working.

There are usually fees for managing the investment.

Limits are set by IRS for yearly contribution totals.

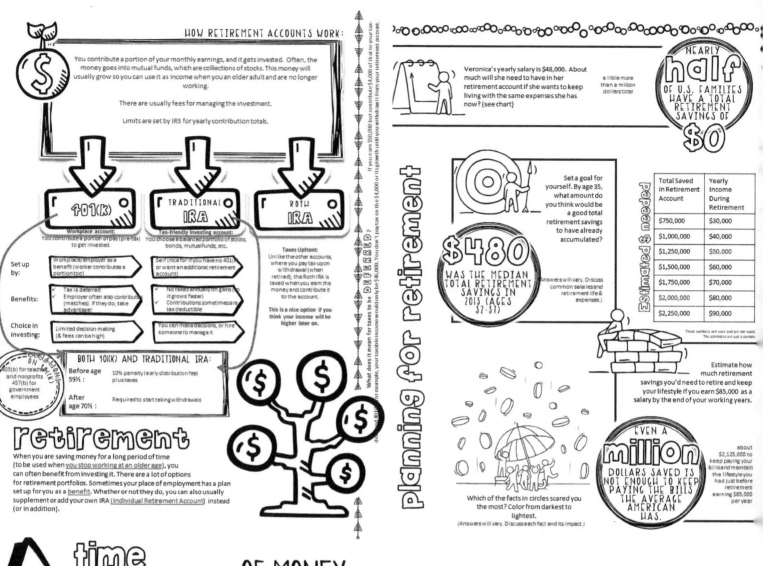

401(K)
Workplace account:
You contribute a portion of pay (pre-tax) to get invested.

TRADITIONAL IRA
Tax-friendly investing account:
You choose a balanced portfolio of stocks, bonds, mutual funds, etc.

ROTH IRA
Taxes Upfront:
Unlike the other accounts, where you pay tax upon withdrawal (when retired), the Roth IRA is taxed when you earn the money and contribute it to the account.

This is a nice option if you think your income will be higher later on.

Set up by:
- Workplace/employer as a benefit (worker contributes a portion too)
- Self (nice for if you have no 401k or want an additional retirement account)

Benefits:
- Tax is deferred
- Employer often also contributes (matches). If they do, take advantage!
- No taxes annually on gains (so it grows faster)
- Contributions sometimes are tax deductible

Choice in investing:
- Limited decision making (& fees can be high)
- You can make decisions, or hire someone to manage it

VARIATIONS ON IRA: 403(b) for teachers and nonprofits 457(b) for government employees

BOTH 401(K) AND TRADITIONAL IRA:
Before age 59½: 10% penalty (early distribution fee) plus taxes
After age 70½: Required to start taking withdrawals

retirement

When you are saving money for a long period of time (to be used when you stop working at an older age), you can often benefit from investing it. There are a lot of options for retirement portfolios. Sometimes your place of employment has a plan set up for you as a benefit. Whether or not they do, you can also usually supplement or add your own IRA (Individual Retirement Account) instead (or in addition).

What does it mean for taxes to be DEFERRED?

If you earn $50,000 but contribute $4,000 of that to your tax-deferred 401(k) or IRA, your taxable income would only be $46,000. You don't pay tax on the $4,000 or its growth until you withdraw it from your retirement account.

Planning for retirement

Veronica's yearly salary is $48,000. About much will she need to have in her retirement account if she wants to keep living with the same expenses she has now? (see chart)

a little more than a million dollars total

NEARLY **half** OF U.S. FAMILIES HAVE A TOTAL RETIREMENT SAVINGS OF **$0**

Set a goal for yourself. By age 35, what amount do you think would be a good total retirement savings to have already accumulated?

$480 WAS THE MEDIAN TOTAL RETIREMENT SAVINGS IN 2013 (AGES 32-37)

Answers will vary. Discuss common salaries and retirement life & expenses.)

	Total Saved in Retirement Account	Yearly Income During Retirement
Estimated $ needed	$750,000	$30,000
	$1,000,000	$40,000
	$1,250,000	$50,000
	$1,500,000	$60,000
	$1,750,000	$70,000
	$2,000,000	$80,000
	$2,250,000	$90,000

These numbers will vary and are not exact. The estimates are just a sample.

Estimate how much retirement savings you'd need to retire and keep your lifestyle if you earn $85,000 as a salary by the end of your working years.

Which of the facts in circles scared you the most? Color from darkest to lightest.
(Answers will vary. Discuss each fact and its impact.)

EVEN A **million** DOLLARS SAVED IS NOT ENOUGH TO KEEP PAYING THE BILLS THE AVERAGE AMERICAN HAS.

about $2,125,000 to keep paying your bills and maintain the lifestyle you had just before retirement earning $85,000 per year

time value OF MONEY

value ← time

Starting investing just a bit younger made a HUGE difference over time!

- started earliest, most $
- late start, but contributing double
- contributing normally

Starting investing as age 35 isn't too late, but the growth at the end is nowhere near as steep as the guy who started just 10 years earlier.

$400,000
$300,000
$200,000
$100,000

Age 25   Age 35   Age 45   Age 55

I started investing for retirement too late in life, so I contributed DOUBLE each month but STILL can't win!

Label the axes. In each pencil, give the details shown for each investor's situation. In the speech bubbles, explain the results and impact of the decisions he / she made. Color code to match the profiles below.

Note: Growth is slow at first, but then the curve gets steeper over time. The FINAL 10 years is where Lem wins out by such a drastic amount compared to M'Kayla. That is the time value of money at work.

Use the graph to estimate the value in each account at age 65:

superstar EARLY INVESTOR
~$450,000

playing catch-up INVESTOR WILL REGRETS
~$240,000

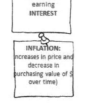
out of time DOUBLING DOWN & STILL BEHIND
~$330,000

Lem knows the time value of money. Every small amount he invests early is worth much more later on. His early start on his retirement account at age 25 pays off. He never had to put in more than he could manage easily, but he still ends up with the most value.

M'Kayla does what many adults do, setting up her investment accounts at age 35. Although the short delay does not seem significant, the fact that she started later than Lem means that she will never achieve the same value in her account.

Roger realizes he is late to the game, and starts investing in his retirement account at age 40. He puts in **double** what the others invest, straining his daily income just to make ends meet as he tries to make up for his delay, but he still cannot make up for the lost time to match what Lem did with small, easy contributions.

Each $1 NOW is essentially worth MORE in the future.

WHY?

Potential for earning INTEREST

INFLATION: (Increases in price and decrease in purchasing value of $ over time)

AUDIO LECTURE & FULL SIZE COLORED SAMPLES FOR EACH PAGE ARE AVAILABLE AT:

MATHGIRAFFE.COM/ SUPPLEMENT

Taxes: the big picture

Create a flow chart: How does a tax system work?
(Flow charts will vary, but should represent this concept): Individuals in a society owe a certain portion of their own money to the government. These payments are required, and can be enforced by the government. The funds then go to cover the government's expenses that in turn benefit the public.

Make a bulleted list: Types of Tax Americans Pay
Sales tax on purchases, **Income tax** on wages earned from working, **Property tax** for your home, **Estate tax** when assets are transferred to heirs upon death, **Payroll tax** as a percent of salary, **Excise tax** on certain purchases like gasoline and alcohol, and even **Gift tax** on gifts!

Doodle some examples: Where does the money go?
(Examples will vary. Students can draw roads, government buildings, garbage trucks, etc.)

Those who have more income are taxed at a higher percent than those with lower income. The rich contribute more tax than the poor.

Explain what is meant by **Progressive Tax**

In the United States, we have a "progressive" income tax structure.

EXPENSES   INCOME

a closer look at Sales Tax

Try calculating sales tax: Find the sales tax and total cost of each purchase in a state that has 8% income tax. Remember to convert the percent to a decimal.

Sales tax rates vary _____ throughout the country.

1 backpack
$67.99
$67.99 (.08) = $5.44 tax
$73.43 total

4 books
$18 (.08) = $1.44 tax
$19.44 total

To find 8% of $67.99, multiply .08 by $67.99

Depending on where a worker lives, income tax may have to be paid on a _____ level federal _____ level, and even sometimes a local level.

The agency responsible for collecting federal tax and enforcing federal tax laws for the United States is called the:

Internal Revenue Service

a closer look at Income Tax

Define each, and label it in the flowchart.

W2: A form that shows the entire year's income and withholdings that is used to file federal and state taxes for the year

W4: A form that you complete when you are hired (or when you want to adjust it) that tells your employer how much to withhold from each paycheck to send as federal tax.

1040: A form that you complete at the end of each tax year to show your income and deductions, file your annual federal taxes, and determine any tax you owe or need refunded

Paycheck: The wages you receive from your employer for work you've done (accompanied by a stub that shows withholdings as well)

Tax withheld: Portion of your paycheck you don't receive that goes directly from your employer to the government

Income Taxes

You OWE money at tax time if... the amount that your employer withheld and already paid in tax is LESS than your tax responsibility calculated on your 1040

You RECEIVE refund money at tax time if... the amount your employer withheld and already paid in tax is GREATER than your tax responsibility calculated on your 1040

Employee will either owe more money in taxes or receive a refund.

Color code the words "employee" and "employer" as you fill in the blanks.

Employee fills out a W4

Employee receives a pay stub showing how much was withheld

Employer uses the w4 to determine how much of each paycheck to withhold.

The money that was withheld is sent directly from the Employer to the government.

At tax time, the _____ sends each worker a W2 that shows the year's income and withholdings.

Employee files his/her taxes using form 1040 and referencing the W2 along with other documents.

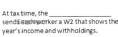

Filing Your TAXES

withholdings
sometimes need to be adjusted and are based on:
- marital status
- withholding allowances claimed
- any exemptions from withholding
- additional amount you may want withheld

deductions
are amounts that can be subtracted from your income before calculating tax.
Examples:
(Student lists or sketches may vary)
Home mortgage interest
Medical expenses
Charitable gifts
etc.

dependents
a person who relies on someone else for income (like a minor child)
(Students can sketch children / babies)

tax brackets & tax tables
Once you have calculated your taxable income and accounted for deductions, you use a chart called a tax table to determine how much tax you should have paid for the year.

Sample Tax Table
Note: The taxpayer is charged in increments, so in this example, the first $20,000 of a married couple's income would be taxed at 10%, then their income from there up to $70,000 would be taxed at 12% and so on. The real tax table you'll reference each year is much more detailed in order to calculate all this for you.

	Taxable Income (Single)	Taxable Income (Married Filing Jointly)
10%	Less than $9,500	Less than $20,000
12%	$9,500 to $35,000	$20,000 to $70,000
16%	$35,001 to $70,000	$70,001 to $100,000
19%	$70,001 to $100,000	$100,001 to $140,000
23%	$100,001 to $145,000	$140,001 to $200,000
27%	$145,001 to $200,000	$200,001 to $300,000
32%	$200,001 to	$300,001 to

What is the top tax rate would a married couple filing jointly (together) have to pay on a taxable income of $152,700?
23% max

What is the highest tax rate would a single person have to pay on a taxable income of $41,250?
16% max

Explain this difference.
In a progressive tax system, those with higher income pay a higher percentage of their income.

Shade / color ALL the % tax rows that will apply to some portion of the married couple's tax calculation based on the note at the top.

What about BUSINESS?

A business is taxed on its **profit** rather than on income, like an individual person is taxed.

revenue → expenses → profit

revenue — total amount of money coming into the business (from sales or other income)

expenses — money paid out for the ordinary costs of doing business

profit — what's left; the overall financial gain (or loss if it's negative!)

calculating profits

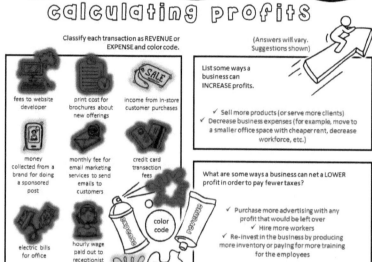

Classify each transaction as REVENUE or EXPENSE and color code.

- fees to website developer
- print cost for brochures about new offerings
- income from in-store customer purchases
- money collected from a brand for doing a sponsored post
- monthly fee for email marketing services to send emails to customers
- credit card transaction fees
- electric bills for office
- hourly wage paid out to receptionist

color code

(Answers will vary. Suggestions shown)

List some ways a business can INCREASE profits.

- ✓ Sell more products (or serve more clients)
- ✓ Decrease business expenses (for example, move to a smaller office space with cheaper rent, decrease workforce, etc.)

What are some ways a business can net a LOWER profit in order to pay fewer taxes?

- ✓ Purchase more advertising with any profit that would be left over
- ✓ Hire more workers
- ✓ Re-invest in the business by producing more inventory or paying for more training for the employees

how it works

The individual (or business) and insurance company have an agreement or contract, where the payments made will transfer a large portion of financial burden for covered situations onto the insurance company.

In case of a covered event, the individual will receive payment from the insurance company. (If not, they will not generally get their money back. You pay for insurance "just in case."

I choose to purchase insurance because...

...I can afford the monthly fees, but I know I would not be able to afford the much larger total cost of a catastrophe. The fact that I am covered and don't have to worry is worth paying for, whether or not I ever get my money back.

INSURANCE — helps protect people financially from risk

goal

Goal: protect myself and everything I value from the financial cost of an unexpected emergency situation.

group "pool" effect

- paying monthly for a policy
- paying monthly for a policy

ONLY ONE HAVING A PAYOUT FROM AN INSURANCE CLAIM THIS YEAR

Many different people pay into insurance policies. The system works when only a small percent of those people will need to be paid back by the insurance company at any time. In a way, participants are pooling their money to minimize risk.

- paying monthly for a policy
- paying monthly for a policy
- paying monthly for a policy

risk management

Everyone is subject to some RISK just by being alive.

Insurance is one way to minimize the impact of those risks.

People insure their homes, their valuables, their vehicles, their lives for the sake of their loved ones, and even their pets!

Insurance companies use probability and the large number of customers to minimize their own risk. It's very unlikely that many people will make a claim at the same time, and they account for the possible situations and how likely each outcome will be before setting prices.

Strategy and Probability

INSURANCE

Policy — The contract that lays out your insurance plan. It describes what is covered and how much you'll be paid in the event of a claim on a covered situation.

Premium — The amount that you pay for the insurance policy to be in effect (often paid monthly or yearly)

Beneficiary — (Sketches will vary – students represent each term with a picture.) The person who receives the money (in the case of a life insurance policy, the spouse or children often get the benefit if the policyholder dies.)

Term — The time period that your policy covers

Deductible — A specific amount that your plan requires you to pay before the insurance company will give any money. (This will vary and is known upfront.)

coverage
The amount that you can receive (maximum) in benefits if you do have a claim for a particular event.

risk
The probability of an insured situation actually occurring

claim
An official request made to the insurance company notifying them that a covered event has occurred and you would like payment

rider
An added clause that you can tack on to your policy to provide more than a standard / basic protection package.

KEY TERMS

---

main types of INSURANCE

protecting against Death & Sickness — life & health
- life insurance
  - TERM life ins.
  - WHOLE LIFE
- health insurance

protecting Assets (both property and financial) — property & casualty
- auto
- home
- other property
- disaster
- misc. (travel, pet, etc.)

a little history
The concept of "insurance" was actually developed by the ancient ___Babylonians___. The merchants sometimes bought insurance policies on purchased goods that they were still waiting for. If delivery did not occur, the insurance would give them back the lost money.

Life and health insurance policies protect people from... financial loss due to illness, premature death, or other medical / health related costs and complications

casualty insurance — protects you from liability claims
both guard you from losing money
property insurance — protects your STUFF (assets)

---

home owners insurance

explain it
Homeowners purchase an insurance policy that they pay for consistently to cover them in case of loss of property or liability claims related to the home, property, or belongings.

What happens if you make a claim
If the home or belongings inside are damaged, the insurance company usually will first investigate to verify (or have you send photos, proof, etc.) and then will pay to have them fixed or replaced.

list some factors
That can impact the cost of your home insurance
- Crime rates and home prices in the neighborhood
- Construction, materials, square footage, and features of the home
- Distance to fire hydrant/station or police station

label what's covered
- **structure** — the actual house (the building)
- **belongings** — all your personal property
- **liability** — cost if someone else is harmed on your property, or by your pet, etc.

doodle the dangers — What can damage homes?
student doodles will vary. Examples: tornado, fire, thieves, hail, gas explosion...

renters insurance
A renter lives on property owned by someone else (a landlord), who would be responsible for insuring the actual building.

Renters insurance covers the renter's belongings (property like furniture, personal items, etc.) as well as any liability of the individual renter as a tenant. (Liability coverage is for when there is an accident, injury, etc. that the renter is held responsible for legally.)

AUTO insurance

Collision Coverage — reimburses you for repairs to your car after an accident

Liability Insurance — covers you when you and your actions are responsible for an accident

Comprehensive Coverage — is for financial losses due to occurrences other than collisions / accidents. (weather damage, theft, etc.)

Personal Injury Protection — is available in some states and covers medical bills for all people in the car after an accident, no matter who is at fault

Uninsured Motorist Coverage — Although it is usually illegal to drive without insurance, some people still do. This protection helps with expenses when the driver responsible for an accident does not have enough insurance.

it's the law!
Almost all states require drivers to be insured. However, the types of coverage required vary from one state to another. Some only require liability insurance, while others require more.

Keeping your costs low:
- Keep good driving record
- Increase deductible
- Shop around / bundle with same company as your home insurance

liability — legal responsibility for others' property or bodily harm

property — damage / theft

medical — cost of treatment for injuries (and sometimes even lost income / funeral costs)

Get discounts for driving safely

insurance

LIFE insurance

You pay your regular premiums for your policy, and in return, the insurance company will:

give money to your beneficiaries / people depending on you when/if you die.

How you benefit

You can be sure that your loved ones will be ok financially if you die and they no longer have the income or care that you provide. They can use the money for your funeral expenses, to pay off any debt, replace your income, pay the bills, etc.

How the insurance company benefits

PROFITS:
- ✓ investing the premium that you pay.
- ✓ Charging enough (by calculating each person's risk) to make more than they have to pay in claims.
- ✓ Never having to pay out to people who stop payments (lapsed policies), since they already made money from those people.

2 main types

term
life insurance

$

- less expensive
- only in effect for a certain time period
- based on probability that the person will die within that next set number of years
- Money is gone (your family does not get anything back) if you don't die in that term.

whole life / permanent
life insurance

$$$

- more expensive
- also includes long-term savings
- All the money put in throughout the years is not just lost / gone forever if you don't die within the term.

Many life insurance companies require... health screenings to assess your risk (probability of death) before they calculate your cost (premium).

Medical bills are the **#1** cause of U.S. bankruptcies.

All humans should get health insurance.

The cost of medical bills after a serious unexpected health emergency can ruin your financial life forever.

Who needs it?

FAMILIES can often share a health insurance plan and get coverage as a family.

STUDENTS can sometimes stay on their parents' health insurance plan even into the college years, depending on age, the laws, and individual circumstances.

What's covered?

Label 3 types of care. Give examples.

- sickness
- (Student examples will vary.)
- injury
- preventative care

Costs you may still have
in addition to your premium payments for the plan

out of pocket limit – ...most you'll ever have to pay in a year

deductible – amount you'll pay out of pocket before insurance kicks in

copay – amount you pay when you need a specific appointment, health service, or medication

Try it

Geena went in for a doctor appointment, and then they sent her for a diagnostic scan. Her insurance covers the entire doctor visit except for a $10 copay. It also covers 30% of the $350.75 bill for the scan before her deductible is met. (If her deductible for the year *has* been met, the scan will be covered 100%.) She then needs to pick up a prescription that has a total cost of $75.50. With her insurance plan, she only pays a $15 copay for medications. On this particular plan, the copays must be made whether or not the deductible has been met. Find her total cost for this medical situation if she *has* meet her deductible for the year, and her cost if she has not yet.

Before deductible is met for the year:
$10 + $245.53 + $15
$270.53

If she has already met it
$10 + $15
= $25

Sometimes, a full time job comes with benefits that include health insurance. Your employer may have a **group plan** (that they pay a percent of) that employees can take advantage of. A portion of the cost for that is generally withdrawn from your paycheck if you choose to participate.
- cheaper if employer splits cost
- less choice since employer chose the plan options
- contributions are not taxed

employer provided health insurance

Vision benefits can often be ADDED ON to a medical plan to cover eye exams, glasses, etc.

If your employer does not offer medical insurance, or you want to supplement it with additional insurance, or just choose to select your own individual plan instead of participating, you can purchase your own.
- more choice
- can keep your plan even if you change jobs
- can sometimes qualify for help from government to pay for it

individual health insurance

medicare
Available for people ages 65+ or with specific needs & covers:

(A) inpatient (admitted to hospital) charges

(B) outpatient (not staying overnight) charges

(C) alternate plan in connection with private ins. companies

(D) prescription medications

medicaid
is government-aided health coverage for people who qualify as needing it based on low income, children's needs, elderly needs, pregnancy, or disability.

Medicaid can help people pay for doctor visits, hospital bills, and even long-term care like nursing home care or home health care.

Health Maintenance Organization
This type of health care plan:
- Has fewer options for providers
- Requires you to choose a PCP (primary care physician) in the network
- May be slightly less expensive than a PPO
- Requires you to get a referral from your PCP to go to any specialists

Dental benefits are also often an ADD ON to your medical plan to cover dentist visits.

Preferred Provider Organization
This type of health care plan:
- Has more options for care providers
- May offer a network of doctors at one price tier, but still allow you to pay more for doctors outside that network
- Usually is a more expensive plan

HMO | PPO

Specialized insurance

Label these types of "other" insurance. Give examples and/or reasons to purchase each.

Personal valuables
For example: Jewelry, art, precious collections

Some people choose to purchase insurance plans for other things as well. Assets may be worth insuring if they are either:
→ Valuable (worth a lot of money)
→ Unique and irreplaceable

pets
For example: Liability if your pet hurts someone, pet accident illness insurance, pet wellness insurance

tools or equipment
Examples: business equipment like a printing press, valuable technology, power tools

vacation bookings
So you can get a refund on plane tickets, hotel costs, etc. if you cannot go

people and/or body parts
For example: pro sports players, celebrities, owner of a big company

Try it

Sergio is purchasing a new phone that he is paying for over the next 2 years on a monthly payment plan. The clerk offers him a protection plan, which is like a small-scale form of insurance for it. He would add $18.50 to each of his monthly payments, and would then get a free replacement, no questions asked, if it breaks within the first three years. What price would the phone have to be before he ends up paying more for the protection plan than the equivalent replacement phone would even be worth?

Paying $18.50 over 2 years:
$18.50 (24) ≈ $444

Do you think it's worth it?
(Students decide if they think it's worth it.)

fraud & risk

insurability factors

Imagine you work for the insurance company.

You'll decide how prudent it is to insure someone based on their risk profile, health and medical history, accident history, credit score, etc. Depending on the type of insurance they want to buy, you'll look at a variety of different factors to determine the probability of a claim, and therefore the price of the policy.

assess the risk

Color risk factors red. Color traits of an individual you can insure with less risk blue.

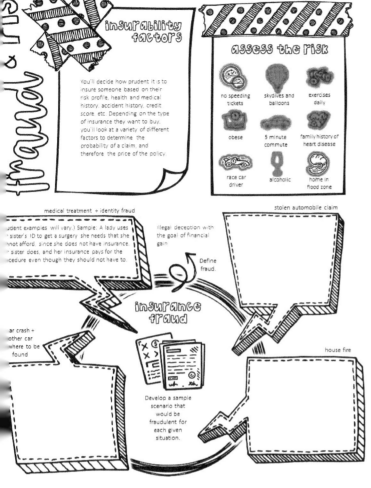

- no speeding tickets
- skydives and balloons
- exercises daily
- obese
- 5 minute commute
- family history of heart disease
- race car driver
- alcoholic
- home in flood zone

insurance fraud

medical treatment + identity fraud

[st]udent examples will vary.) Sample: A lady uses [her] sister's ID to get a surgery she needs that she [can]not afford, since she does not have insurance. [Her] sister does, and her insurance pays for the [pro]cedure even though they should not have to.

Illegal deception with the goal of financial gain

Define fraud.

stolen automobile claim

[c]ar crash + [an]other car [no]where to be found

house fire

Develop a sample scenario that would be fraudulent for each given situation.

AUDIO LECTURE & FULL SIZE COLORED SAMPLES FOR EACH PAGE ARE AVAILABLE AT:

MATHGIRAFFE.COM/ SUPPLEMENT

[Most] Americans take on debt to [buy] their homes, vehicles, [and o]ther large expenses.

[This st]rategy allows them to [borro]w the money to purchase [somet]hing expensive, like a [house], and then slowly pay back [the d]ebt owed on that loan in [small] payments each month.

[But] the catch:
[(INTER]EST) – pay more in the [long r]un than if you had saved up [ahead] of time to pay in cash up [front].

BAD DEBT

- payday loans (taking from NEXT paycheck before it comes)
- taking a loan out of your 401k savings
- credit cards you don't pay the whole balance on every month
- hefty auto loans

give examples

Bad debt is when instead of giving you flexibility / options for repaying, you end up being unable to recover from the debt. In the long run, a bad debt severely damages your financial future. It can start a CYCLE that you are unable to bounce back from, since you are always a few steps behind in your payments and cannot catch up.

Bad debts often have high interest or variable interest rates, but they can also stem from normal credit card debts that are mismanaged (usually by not paying the full monthly amount on time every time).

"3 Cs" OF CREDIT

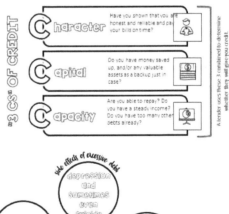

Character — Have you shown that you are honest and reliable and pay your bills on time?

Capital — Do you have money saved up, and/or any valuable assets as a backup just in case?

Capacity — Are you able to repay? Do you have a steady income? Do you have too many other debts already?

A lender uses these 3 combined to determine whether they will give you credit.

credit

receiving items or services before paying in full, with the agreement that payments will be made in the future ("buying on credit")

Why might a person want credit as an option?

They can afford the item in smaller, consistent payments as their monthly income comes in, but cannot buy it upfront in one large sum

Credit score
➤ Changes over time, depending on _how you accumulate debt and/or pay your bills_
➤ Reflects your credit history and your ability to _repay a debt in a timely manner_
➤ Is used by creditors to decide _whether or not to_ _____ _lend you money_

How can you start to build credit?

Get a secured credit card or student credit card, and start making small purchases and paying off the entire balance every single month

Pay rent and utility bills consistently.

---

debt-to-income ratio = total monthly debt payments owed / monthly gross income

GOAL: Keep your debt-to-income ratio less than 15%

define debt
money that is owed / due

Try it: Calculate the debt-to-income ratio for a person who owes $400 for debts each month and earns $2,000 in gross monthly income.

400 / 2000 = 0.2 = 20%

side effects of excessive debt

- depression and sometimes even suicide
- stress
- poor physical health
- difficulty reaching financial goals

loans

How does a loan work?

Once you APPLY, the lender will review your CREDIT and determine whether to lend to you, and set an interest rate. If you sign a loan CONTRACT, you'll then be obligated to pay it back according to the set terms and schedule. You'll pay for this over time as a monthly bill, and end up paying more in the long run because of the interest. If you DEFAULT (don't pay it back), there are negative consequences.

Give examples of some expenses for which people may get a loan.

Student doodles may vary. Examples: home, car, college

doodle it

mortgage

To Buy a House:

- You pay a down payment up front.
- You borrow a loan from the bank. The principal is the amount you need to borrow to purchase the home (the cost minus your down payment.)
- You will then have to pay it back to the bank, a little per month. You will also have to pay them interest. You will also have to pay taxes and insurance each month.
- You will own the home as an asset when your mortgage is paid off (often 30 years later).

Define each key term.

down payment

a percent of the purchase price that you pay up front from your own savings to secure the purchase and get started

interest rate

a percent of the amount borrowed that is owed on top of the principal (initial amount borrowed) in return for the use of the lender's money as a loan

monthly payment

the amount you pay each month for the mortgage principal, mortgage interest, property tax, and homeowner insurance

$32,250 down

$414,000 in payments

$446,250 total

Akio is purchasing a $215,000 home with a 15% down payment. Her monthly mortgage payment is estimated to be an average of $1,150 for 30 years. This includes the taxes and insurance, as a mortgage payment generally does. How much will she pay in total? Write her down payment in one window, the sum of all her monthly payments in another, and the grand total in the front door.

collateral — an asset that is offered as loan security

fixed rate

In a "fixed rate" mortgage, the interest rate is set when you sign the mortgage agreement. You will pay the same % interest throughout the duration of your mortgage payments.

adjustable rate

In an "adjustable rate" mortgage, the interest rate will vary over time. You'll pay different % interest at different times throughout your mortgage payments as the rates adjust.

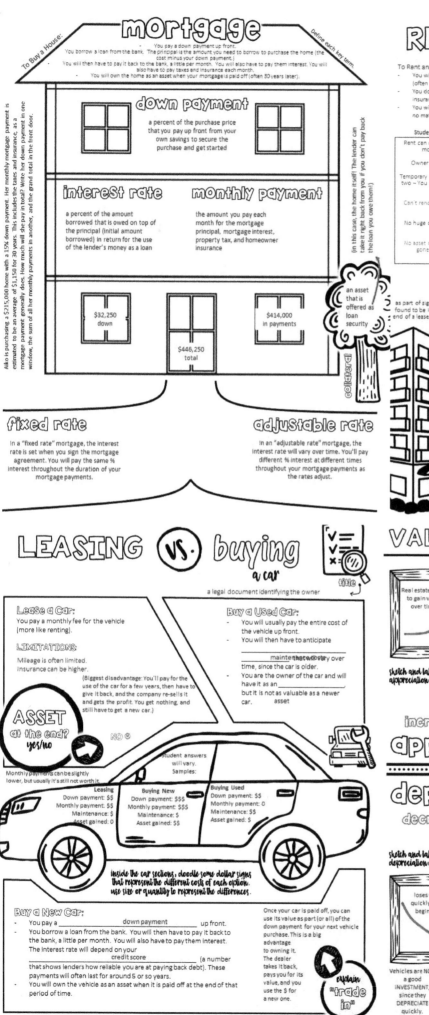

RENTING vs. buying a home

YOU own it!

To Rent an Apartment:

- You will pay a one-time security deposit up front (often one month's rent).
- You do not have to pay homeowner taxes or insurance, but will pay renter's insurance.
- You will not have the property as an asset at the end, no matter how long you pay rent.

Student answers will vary. Samples:

Rent can often be cheaper each month than mortgage payments would be.

Owner pays for maintenance, not you!

Temporary (ok if you need to move in a year or two – You won't lose $ or have to find a buyer for the home)

Can't renovate or change things much – just have to deal with it

No huge down payment (Security deposit is usually much less.)

No asset at the end. Your rent money is just gone, not invested in the property.

ESCROW — homeowner's insurance · escrow is a third party account that holds the funds that will be paid to the lender — *identify what is held in an escrow account* — mortgage principal · mortgage interest · *define it* · property taxes

security deposit

money paid up front as part of signing on for a rental agreement. (If the property is found to be in good condition, you usually get this back at the end of a lease. If not, it is kept by the owner of the property to pay for the damages.)

HOA fees

Fees that are paid in addition to normal monthly costs in certain communities (The money usually goes toward upkeep, landscaping, improvements, community services that all residents of the neighborhood benefit from.)

You own it at the end! Property is a good investment, and an asset.

High cost up front (have to save up a payment first)

Not easy to move around (have to find a buyer, sell the home, and may lose $ if you have not lived there for a few years)

You are responsible for all maintenance

You get to make any changes you want / renovations

Mortgage interest is tax deductible

Landlord owns it. You just pay to live there.

ASSET at the end? yes/no — NO ☹ · YES! ☺

utilities

services like electricity, internet, water, etc. that are paid for in monthly bills (additional cost on top of rent or mortgage payments)

define each term. in the blank, write or doodle some differences between renting and buying. use one corner for advantages, and one for disadvantages.

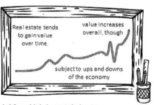

LEASING vs. buying a car

title — a legal document identifying the owner

Lease a Car:

You pay a monthly fee for the vehicle (more like renting).

LIMITATIONS:

Mileage is often limited. Insurance can be higher.

(Biggest disadvantage: You'll pay for the use of the car for a few years, then have to give it back, and the company re-sells it and gets the profit. You get nothing, and still have to get a new car.)

Buy a Used Car:

- You will usually pay the entire cost of the vehicle up front.
- You will then have to anticipate ___maintenance___ that will vary over time, since the car is older.
- You are the owner of the car and will have it as an ___asset___, but it is not as valuable as a newer car.

ASSET at the end? yes/no → NO ☹

Monthly payments can be slightly lower, but usually it's still not worth it.

Student answers will vary. Samples:

	Leasing	Buying New	Buying Used
Down payment:	$$	$$$	$$
Monthly payment:	$$	$$$	0
Maintenance:	$	$	$$
Asset gained:	0	$$	$

inside the car sections, doodle some dollar signs that represent the different costs of each option. use size or quantity to represent the differences.

Buy a New Car:

- You pay a ___down payment___ up front.
- You borrow a loan from the bank. You will then have to pay it back to the bank, a little per month. You will also have to pay them interest. The interest rate will depend on your ___credit score___ (a number that shows lenders how reliable you are at paying back debt). These payments will often last for around 5 or so years.
- You will own the vehicle as an asset when it is paid off at the end of that period of time.

Once your car is paid off, you can use its value as part (or all) of the down payment for your next vehicle purchase. This is a big advantage to owning it. The dealer takes it back, pays you for its value, and you use the $ for a new one.

explain "trade in"

VALUE OF ASSETS OVER TIME

Real estate tends to gain value over time — value increases overall, though — subject to ups and downs of the economy

sketch and label a graph showing appreciation of a house

Property is a good INVESTMENT that APPRECIATES over time.

(student doodles or answers will vary. Examples: gold, stocks, oil, land, bonds)

appreciation
increase in value over time

define it

depreciation
decrease in value over time

in the blank space, draw some other items that appreciate and depreciate.

sketch and label a graph showing depreciation of a vehicle

loses value quickly at the beginning — older cars are worth much less

Vehicles are NOT a good INVESTMENT, since they DEPRECIATE quickly.

(student doodles or answers will vary. Examples: jewelry, electronics, furniture, cell phones, clothing, books, purses, etc.)

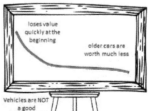

College Costs

Some students choose to go to a lower cost college, community college, or only enter a 2-year program instead of a 4+ year program to save money, or if it fits their plans best. Some students go to a 4 year university. The tuition costs can really add up.

Draft up two different career plans that interest you.

(student answers will vary.)

Next, investigate the education that is required for each.

career

Research a sample college tuition schedule to estimate the costs of your plan, or write up the alternative paths that you may take.

>>>>>>>>>

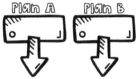

Plan A   Plan B

In order to pay for college education, many students apply for loans. A parent often has to

_____ and be accountable, since students may not yet have credit built up.

(Plans should include tuition costs multiplied by the number of years required for each step/phase of education, and then estimate the final salary to see how it balances out.)

Student loans:

Identify the two main types of interest accrual.

subsidized
Dept. of Education pays interest for you while you are still in college, then it starts accumulating after you graduate.

unsubsidized
interest begins accruing right away when you receive loan money and accumulates while you are still in school.

(a legal agreement between two parties in the case of a loan, it lays out the amount and the terms of repayment, and you have to sign off that you will repay.)

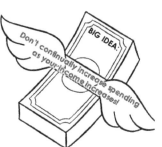

Try It

Assume that a student loan that pays for all 4 years of college will cost a total of $65,680 to pay pack. With payments of $325 per month, how long will it take to repay this loan?

$65680 \div 325 \approx 202$ months

$202 \div 12 \approx 16.8$ years
to pay it off!

WEALTH

❌ is not a matter of how much money is   **earned**

❌ is not a matter of how much money is   **spent**

〰 actually is about how much money is _____   **KEPT**

BIG IDEA:
Don't continually increase spending as your income increases!

income

me spending and most of ...esting / saving goes toward ...ilding ASSETS. Keep this ...tion of your income usage ...her.

Other spending goes toward expenses that will not build wealth. Keep these expenses (the ones that do not become assets) low when you can.

assets

expenses

...ketches will vary. Examples: ...tting some of your income ...ward mutual funds, retirement ...counts, savings, and assets ...at appreciate, such as real ...tate.)

(Sketches will vary. Examples: the portion of income that goes toward paying utility bills, paying off credit card debt, buying a vehicle, spending on personal items like clothes, technology, etc.)

Wealth is not the same as income.
In order to build substantial wealth, more of your income needs to go toward _____
ASSETS
like savings, investments, and purchases that appreciate than the amount of your income that goes toward _____
EXPENSES
like spending, bills, and debt. Include some specific samples inside each circle.

To calculate an individual's
worth

Add up the value of all assets, including things like...

◇ Cash in savings and checking accounts
◇ Money in investment accounts
◇ Car current value
◇ Home current value
◇ Other valuable items, businesses, land owned, etc.

Then subtract the total of any liabilities / debt, such as things like...

◇ Mortgage
◇ Car loan
◇ Student loan
◇ Credit card debt
◇ Any other debt

NET WORTH

NEW YORK   LONDON   MOSCOW

Explain the differences clearly, including a review of their choices and reasoning for the discrepancies despite having the same yearly salary.

try it

Calculate the net worth for each of these two individuals with the same annual income. Which has done a better job of building wealth with the same level of earning?

JOAN
GENERAL CONTRACTOR
AGE 55
SALARY: $95,000

ASSETS:
Cash in all Accounts: $76,000
401k Retirement Funds: $215,000
Home Value: $230,000
Jewelry Collection: $15,000
Vehicle Value: $13,000

ASSETS:
$549,000

DEBTS/LIABILITIES:
Money Owed for Home Mortgage: $64,000
Money Still Owed for Vehicle: $0
Credit Card Debt: $0
Student Loans: $0

LIABILITY:
$64,000

NET WORTH: $485,000

ASSETS:
Cash in all Accounts: $12,000
IRA Retirement Funds: $92,000
Home Value: $305,000
Vehicle Value: $55,000
Rental Property: $123,000

ASSETS:
$587,000

DEBTS/LIABILITIES:
Money Owed for Home Mortgages: $320,000
Money Still Owed for Vehicle: $38,000
Credit Card Debt: $6,500
Student Loans: $27,000

LIABILITY:
$391,500

NET WORTH: $195,500

RODRIGO
PUBLIC SPEAKER & ENTREPRENEUR
AGE 48
AVG. YEARLY INCOME: $95,000

Rodrigo spent more on cars and homes, while saving less for retirement, and he has less cash. Although he owns a lot from all that spending and has a higher total asset value, he still owes a lot for it, so his debt causes his net worth to be lower than Joan's. She has paid things off and not over-spent.

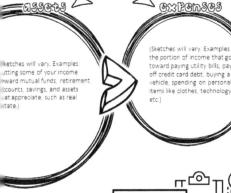

LIFE TIME LINE

Use a color code to mark overlapping ranges on the timeline that represent where you foresee each of these financial "seasons of life" occurring for yourself.

- Education
- Part time job
- Career
- Side gig
- Saving
- Investing
- Retirement

(Students will develop their own color code and the timeline will vary. This is a sample.)

Phases of life

Your financial goals and priorities will (and should) shift throughout the different phases of life.

Identify the 3 key phases of adult life as far as finance, then label them below the timeline.

Working (ACCUMULATION)

Preparing for Retirement (PLANNING)

Legacy (DISTRIBUTION) — You receive retirement income and set up your estate to pass on any leftover funds.

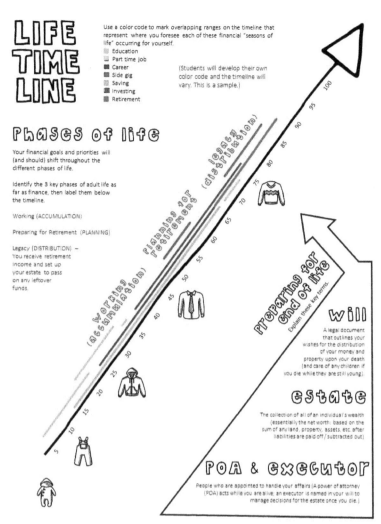

working (accumulation)   planning for retirement (planning)   (legacy distribution)

Preparing for End of life
Explain these key terms.

will
A legal document that outlines your wishes for the distribution of your money and property upon your death (and care of any children if you die while they are still young).

estate
The collection of all of an individual's wealth (essentially the net worth: based on the sum of any land, property, assets, etc. after liabilities are paid off / subtracted out).

POA & executor
People who are appointed to handle your affairs (A power of attorney (POA) acts while you are alive; an executor is named in your will to manage decisions for the estate once you die).

1 Only this portion of the people with high net worth ($3 million +) earns more than $300,000 per year in income!
between $200k and $300k income
> $300k income

2 Only this portion of the people with high net worth ($3 million +) grew up high class.
Grew up middle class
grew up poor

3 Only this portion of The wealth of people with high net worth ($3 million +) came from inheritance.
from earned income
from investments

Some more stats about this group with a net worth of $3 million+ …

On average, they:
- started **saving** at age 14
- started **working** at age 15
- started **giving** to charity and volunteering around age 23
- began **investing** at age 25

BUILDING WEALTH
is possible for people of all income levels and backgrounds

A survey was done back in 2016 to determine common factors between a wide variety of people who were considered to have a HIGH NET WORTH (They had accumulated a net worth of $3 million or more). Create three colored pie charts inside the circles to represent these three inspiring findings. Sum up what struck you about these facts in the box below with a combination of doodles and text.

1 There is a difference between INCOME and WEALTH. 29% of the millionaires surveyed had less than $200K of income per year! In fact, 55% (more than half) had an income of less than 300k per year, yet still built a net worth of more than three million dollars.

2 77 percent of the millionaires surveyed grew up in either poor or middle class families! That 77% breaks down further into a 19% portion who grew up poor, and a 58% portion who grew up in the middle class.

3 These people with high net worth accumulated about half of their overall wealth as earned income. Another 1/3 of their wealth came from investment returns. Only about 10% of the wealth was inherited.

my most inspiring observation from these facts

(Student answers will vary, but should be based upon one or more of the stats.) Sample: You really CAN go from middle/poor class to being a millionaire!

Source: 2016 U.S. Trust Wealth and Worth Survey

KEY CONCEPT

CASH FLOW ANALYSIS

An important part of building wealth is keeping more money than you spend. To do this, be sure to always be aware of your cash flow. This means you are comparing the money coming in to the money going out.

You need your income to always exceed your expenses. Keep track of the funds and be careful that you do not increase your spending faster than you increase your savings.

---

change the world

WEALTH OFFERS OPPORTUNITIES TO SUPPORT CAUSES YOU ARE PASSIONATE ABOUT

Identify one wealthy person who inspires you. Tell why.

(Student answers will vary. Share some examples of people who use their wealth to change the world and support a charity or important causes. Students can doodle a cartoon of the person they choose here.)

IMPACT

List ways that wealthy people can support a cause in ways that other people sometimes cannot. Out of all the possibilities, highlight the ones that appeal most to you. Dream up some ways to use your future wealth to change the world! Use this motivation to learn more about finance, plan for a smart financial future, and prioritize perfecting your habits.

(Answers will vary. Offer suggestions like the following)

- sit on the board as a board member to help make decisions
- donate money
- volunteer (since they may have free time they don't need to spend working at this point)
- start a nonprofit
- run a business that employs like-minded people
- invest in companies that promote the goals
- mentor others

Highlight the icons that represent your own passions that you support already and you'd prioritize if you were able to build significant wealth. Use the empty spaces to add your own additional causes that you feel will change the world, but require resources, funding, time, and energy.

(Student answers will vary.)

---

first steps

WHAT CAN TEENS AND YOUNG ADULTS DO?

TOWARD FINANCIAL STABILITY

Throughout all steps:
>> Continue to increase savings and long-term investments as income grows.
>> Avoid unnecessary _____ debt

In the thought bubbles, sketch or write some overall priorities that you may have at each early phase of financial planning.

(Student answers will vary.) Examples: paying for college, choosing a career path, purchasing a car

(Student answers will vary.) Examples: getting married, starting a career, starting a family, setting up a retirement account, purchasing different types of insurance, buying a home

teen approximately age 12-17

adult approximately age 18-25

LEARNING (adult)
>> Make decisions about insurance.
>> Learn how to file your own taxes.

ACTION (adult)
>> Start a retirement ___ account.
>> Adjust your budget as your expenses and income change.

LEARNING (teen)
>> Make decisions about continuing education, and attend college if it is in your plans.
>> Investigate housing and vehicle purchasing options in your area and in accordance with the financial outlook of your planned career and salary.

ACTION (teen)
>> Start an emergency _____ fund.
>> Get a part time job.
>> Make a _____ budget

LEARNING
>> Get an education, including a high school diploma.
>> Learn the basics of finance as you prepare to become financially independent.
>> Research student loans.

ACTION
>> Open a savings account if you don't have one yet.
>> Open a _____ checking account
>> Get a student credit card.

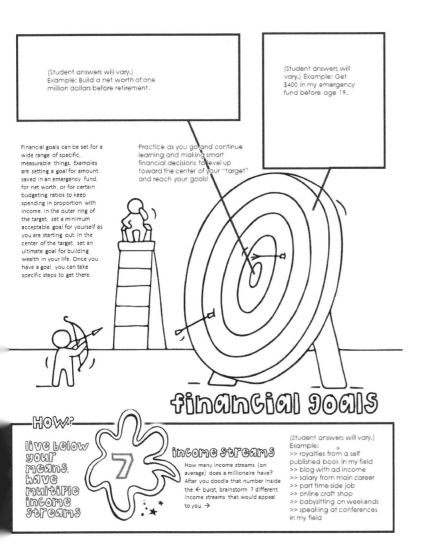

(Student answers will vary.)
Example: Build a net worth of one million dollars before retirement.

(Student answers will vary.) Example: Get $400 in my emergency fund before age 19.

Financial goals can be set for a wide range of specific, measurable things. Examples are setting a goal for amount saved in an emergency fund, for net worth, or for certain budgeting ratios to keep spending in proportion with income. In the outer ring of the target, set a minimum acceptable goal for yourself as you are starting out. In the center of the target, set an ultimate goal for building wealth in your life. Once you have a goal, you can take specific steps to get there.

Practice as you go and continue learning and making smart financial decisions to level up toward the center of your "target" and reach your goals!

financial goals

HOW?

live below your means, have multiple income streams

7

income streams

How many income streams (on average) does a millionaire have? After you doodle that number inside the ← burst, brainstorm 7 different income streams that would appeal to you. →

(Student answers will vary.)
Example:
>> royalties from a self published book in my field
>> blog with ad income
>> salary from main career
>> part time side job
>> online craft shop
>> babysitting on weekends
>> speaking at conferences in my field

AUDIO LECTURE & FULL SIZE COLORED SAMPLES FOR EACH PAGE ARE AVAILABLE AT:

MATHGIRAFFE.COM/ SUPPLEMENT

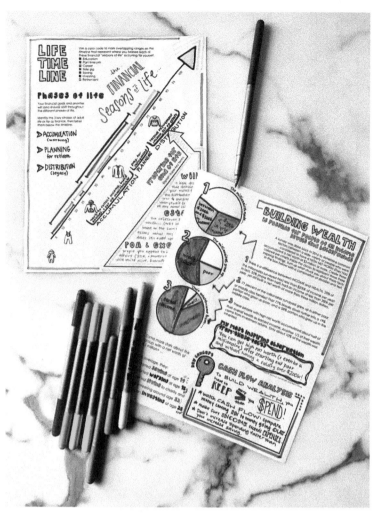

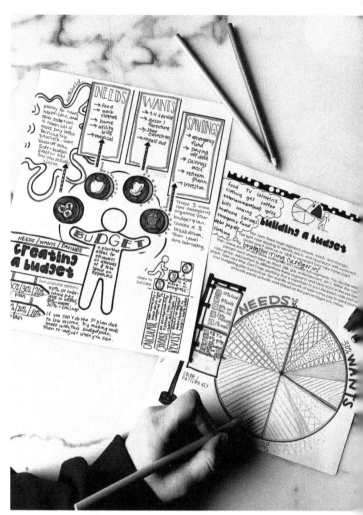

CPSIA information can be obtained
at www.ICGtesting.com
Printed in the USA
LVHW021939050122
707926LV00009B/342